Discovery Trails

DISCOVERY TRAILS

BY

VERA LINDA MELLOR

Vera L Mellor
May 2007

Printed by: Heaton Press, Stockport.
Maps by Vera Linda Mellor and local artist.

Illustrations by local artist, Bronwen Matthews and another local artist who wishes to remain anonymous.

With some financial support from Peak Park Sustainable Development Fund.

ABOUT THE AUTHOR

I will now introduce myself. I am Vera Linda Mellor, originally from Alderley Edge, Cheshire. For the past 27 years I have been resident in the High Peak area, formerly in Chapel-en-le-Frith and, for nearly the last 7 years, in New Mills so I should soon qualify for native status! I am a widow with two adult daughters who have special needs but have achieved a great deal in sport and community activities against formidable odds so I'm extremely proud of them both. In different ways they both share my enthusiasm for the countryside, travel and environmental issues. I have always been keenly interested in supporting local clubs, societies and community groups and am a member of several within High Peak/Disley area. Eventually I hope to become established as a local freelance writer and artist as, in the latter instance, painting in acrylics and mixed medium such as pastels/chalks, calligraphic pens is a favourite hobby of mine.

CONTENTS

6	Romantic trail from The Cat & Fiddle Inn
15	Along the towpath where bridges & banks have tales to tell
29	Hayfield Moorland Taster
36	Two inns, a canal, a former railway, a transformed coal mine site- altogether a best value ramble
47	Lose, Hope or Win
53	The Rosehill-Wyevale Experience
60	High Life! Over the tops at Glossop
66	Round a Staffordshire Moorland Gem
73	Little Hayfield moorland taster
78	Meandering along the Goyt Way to Mouseley Bottom & the Goytside Meadows Nature Reserve
86	Around Hope
94	Interesting Facts About Buxton, High Peaks Historic Spa Town

Copyright - *Vera Linda Mellor 2004*

All rights reserved. No reproduction of this publication permitted without the prior permission of the author.

Whilst very effort has been made to ensure that the information contained in this book is correct on going to print, the author cannot accept responsibility for any omissions or inaccuracies contained therein. Changes in routes or tourist attractions can sometimes occur during or after publication. However I am conscientious about the details involved with the walks are kept as up to date as possible and would welcome any new information from readers that could be relevant to future editions or similar publications.

Discovery Trails

Introduction

As with my first book "Rambler's Diary" which described my experiences of short rambles in and around the Peak District, this next one is also a celebration of the many curiosities, beautiful and special things found in our countryside to interest and delight visitors and local people alike.

Like "Rambler's Diary" most of the walks featured in these articles are intended for people who, for various reasons, prefer to do shorter walks which can often be every bit as enjoyable, interesting, and worthwhile as their longer counterparts, as well as being more convenient to fit in during a day out, weekend or as part of a holiday itinery.

As with my first book, this second one "Discovery Trails" is also intended to be an appreciation of our beautiful countryside, its wildlife including flowers, plants and trees, its often weird and quirky rock formations and its local history.

However, "Discovery Trails" contains more detailed information about facilities for disabled people to enable them to make informed choices about planning their countryside outings and gaining easier, more convenient access to country beauty spots and local places of interest. Several access groups have recently been formed around the High Peak area, at New Mills, Glossop, Buxton and Hope to campaign for better planned and designed walking/cycling/wheelchair routes and footpaths which disabled people can use confidently. To liase with local authorities and other relevant organisations in order to achieve these aims is, of course, an important part of their activities. Information about these groups is available from volunteer centres, community centres, heritage and leisure centres, health centres and some clinics.

There are so many organisations, information services and individuals to whom I'm greatly obliged for supplying interesting facts and detailed information required in order to produce this book. In addition, two local artists, Bronwen Matthews (Disley Art Society) and another one who wishes to remain anonymous and who gave me some useful tips on producing good maps, have most kindly done excellent illustrations and I am taking this opportunity to thank them most profoundly for their cheerful, enthusiastic co-operation. They are all mentioned, including the reference literature used, in my list of acknowledgments on the back page.

Finally here are a few points to bear in mind to ensure happy, trouble-free country rambles. Always wear either walking boots or substantial flat shoes if your walk is likely to take you over any rough or muddy terrain. Even in summer, always take a waterproof garment with you, in case of unpredictable wet weather occurring. If footpaths lead over farmland, always close any gates behind you to prevent farmers from losing livestock. If you have young children with you, it's wise to take a small first aid kit along in case of any minor accidents. For motorists: If you park your car and then go walking, for peace of mind, always remember to lock your car and also lock away any valuables in your boot especially at popular beauty spots, country parks/trails during the usual walking season.

Romantic Trail from the Cat & Fiddle Inn

Distances: Cat & Fiddle to Errwood Hall (ruin) in the Goyt Valley – 2 1/4 miles by easy going path. To Bunsall Cob (old railway track) from Errwood car park – 1.5 miles.

Facilities: Picnic site and toilets (inc disabled) at Derbyshire Bridge car park. Ranger Service point also here. Picnic sites and car parks at Errwood Reservoir, The Street (next facility straight on along reservoir shore) and Bunsal Cob. Also car parks at Goyts Lane (when approaching the valley from Buxton), Pym Chair (short distance from Cat's Tor) and viewpoint on route from Whaley Bridge and just below concessionary Horse Route at Fernilee Reservoir.

Refreshments available from vans which are usually in the valley's car parks. Cat & Fiddle offer lunches and evening meals are also available.

Cycle paths are dotted around Fernilee Reservoir and at Goyts Lane car park there is an area of easy access routes for use by disabled people (be careful when crossing the road there). The old railway track where the former Cromford & High Peak Railway used to run has a level surface and panoramic moorland views to admire en route.

Public transport links: Buses: **61** Bowers Glossop to Buxton service. Stops on Long Hill Rd on right-hand side – look out for clearly signposted entrance to the Goyt Valley. Daily service. Sometimes Yorkshire Traction Co takes over at weekends, Sundays and Bank Holidays.

58 Bowers Bakewell-Macclesfield via Buxton-stops at Cat & Fiddle weekdays and weekends including Bank Holidays (no Good Friday service).

Motorists: Take the A5004 from Whaley Bridge (Long Hill Rd) to Fernilee hamlet, look out for Goyt Valley sign on right-hand side and descend the steep minor road. This was the route of the Bunsal Cob incline, one of the four used by the old Cromford & High Peak Railway.

Important Note A one-way system is in operation at all times on the A537 road from Buxton, between Derbyshire Bridge and Errwood. On Sundays and Bank Holidays (between 10.30am -5.30 pm) from 1st May to end of September, the road from The Street car park, leading to Derbyshire Bridge is closed to vehicular traffic except for emergency services, Ranger Service land rovers and special permit holders. However walkers, cyclists and horse riders are allowed to use it.

On a bright, clear, sunny but breezy, cold day in early spring during the late 1990's the Peak Park Rangers, my friendly co-walkers and I, after enjoying a most welcome morning cuppa and biscuits at what was then the canteen in the old Devonshire Royal Hospital, were driven in our community mini-bus from Buxton to the starting point of our walk, the Cat & Fiddle Inn. On this route, the A537 road winds along a most spectacular scenic area via Derbyshire Bridge with its car park and picnic site commanding panoramic moorland views. From Derbyshire Bridge you can see Goyt's Moss, a hollow spot where there was once a large colliery and Deep Clough, a dramatic, narrow, steep-sided, natural tunnel. It's indeed a dramatic landscape of ravines with crystal clear, shining streams, steep "hanging valleys" and heathery, gorse-speckled moorland in between. Our ranger leader pointed out that the source of the River Goyt originates from this moorland area. Some people believe the Goyt is the River Mersey's true source, as it eventually joins the Mersey at Stockport. We felt most privileged to have the opportunity to admire these wonderful views on our journey up to the Cat & Fiddle Inn. Incidentally, this road eventually leads to Macclesfield.

Our walk started from this road's most famous landmark, the Cat & Fiddle. This popular moorland pub is situated in an elevated position 1,690 ft above sea level, the second highest inn in England. Panoramic views over several counties can be seen from here on clear days. This inn was built at the end of the 18th century by Mr J Ryle, a wealthy banker from Macclesfield who, in those days, also owned the moors upon which this remote hostelry was built. Its purpose was for the use of travellers on the turnpike road between Buxton and Manchester. There are several theories as to how it acquired its name but no one knows for sure. The well known nursery rhyme would seem to suggest a logical explanation as its mountainous position would lead one to joke that the place is indeed high enough for a cow to jump over the moon!

It's not hard to imagine that an inn situated in such a wild place would be a bleak spot in winter, subject to severe weather conditions. In Victorian times the inn certainly received some battering during the rough winters which prevailed in those days. In 1879 a severe gale blew the roof off the inn and swept it away onto the moor. Thirteen years later, in the winter of 1892, a huge build-up of snow and ice made it impossible to open the front door or indeed, any of the windows for seven weeks. Even after all that time, an axe and pick were needed to open the door! Nevertheless, the inn has always been a haven for weary travellers of olden and modern times alike for welcome rest, refreshment and a warm up should cold weather prevail.

As with most rivers which develop on high moorland where extremely damp peat-based soil soaks up rain water like a vast sponge, surplus water drains into gullies and then overflows into shiny, silvery trickles, tumbling over crags and boulders, the Goyt likewise tumbles in a relentless rush down to the rocky ravines of Stake, Shooters, Deep and Berry Clough. We were all treated to such a splendid sight as the Goyt's rushing streams leaping over dark grey boulders, surrounded by pink and purple heather-covered moors, to our left, close by Shooter's Clough, as we made our way down the relatively smooth, "easy going path" towards Errwood Reservoir. The added bonus, in the distance, to the left, was the spectacular view of Shining Tor which, as its name suggests, looks like a gleaming pyramid when the sun shines directly on it. Again, in the distance, to the right of our path and lower down in the valley was an equally impressive view of Goytsclough Quarry and Goytsbridge. The latter, the famous packhorse bridge, a favourite spot for photography enthusiasts and artists alike, was originally dismantled when the Errwood and Fernilee Reservoirs were built and then re-constructed over the river, near the quarry.

Goytsclough Quarry has a very interesting history. Now you don't usually associate Pickfords, our country's most famous removal company with wild moorland places. However the quarry was first activated by Thomas Pickford, originally from Adlington, near

Macclesfield who had his land confiscated by Parliament after the English Civil War of 1645 for trading with the Royalists and so, in order to overcome financial loss, he bought the quarry and started a business in road maintenance. A couple of lucrative contracts to provide flagstones for pavement construction, one of which was from London to supply two of their famous streets, Regent and Oxford St, ensured the firm's continuing expansion and prosperity through the next century. Trains of packhorses transported the slabs via Leek to London. James Pickford's London-Manchester Waggoner had depots at Blossoms Inn and the Bell Inn at Wood St, Cheapside, the latter named co-incidentally the same district where Sir Thomas More, the famous Lord Chancellor and Catholic martyr in Henry Vlll's reign, was executed. James Pickford experienced somewhat better luck in Cheapside than the ex-Lord Chancellor did! The packhorse service was very efficient in that, after transporting the slabs, they returned with goods for local towns and villages. Altogether Pickfords was and still is indeed a phenomenal success story.

A few yards from this quarry, Goytsclough Mill and three millworkers cottages once stood. The mill was powered by a water wheel rotated by the fast flowing stream from Stake Clough. The advent of steam power must have gradually ended its function as a mill as it was converted into a paint factory which employed a small workforce. It closed around 1890. The building and cottages have long since gone and the only evidence left of industry is a few stone steps which led up to the waterwheel. There's a car park here now for visitors' convenience. For really intrepid ramblers there's a fairly steep climb up to the summit of Shining Tor via a track which winds round to the left of the quarry with Stakeside on the right.

We continued down the path on our way to Errwood Reservoir. It wound through mixed woodland of oak, birch, and rowan blended with occasional clumps of more exotic trees like Sitka spruce and extra tall Lodgepole pines. Our packed lunches were consumed in the usual friendly atmosphere with the added bonus of shelter from the chilly wind on this bright but wintry day. As you proceed along any of the paths to the reservoir, notice ruts and marks still visible on the paths from carts known as wagons pulled by packhorses prior to the Goyt Valley section of the Cromford & High Peak Railway being completed in 1830. However, in the early days of this railway, steam engines were just used on the steep inclines, providing the power for the trains to negotiate them and the horses were still used to pull the waggons and carriages along the level sections. Later on steam locomotives were used for the whole journey of High Peak Railway from Whaley Bridge to Cromford in South Derbyshire.

We stopped to admire the beauty of Errwood Reservoir, especially as the day was so clear. Then we retraced our steps, ascending the track leading upwards from the picnic area within Errwood car park to the picturesque ruins of what was once the valley's grand Victorian mansion namely Errwood Hall. Even the ruins, in my view, still possessed a poignant, noble, majestic appearance and, some of our party including myself, let our imagination run riot, visualising what the place would have been like in its heyday. We also admired its still beautiful grounds, full of rhododendrons and azalea bushes plus thick coniferous woodlands.

A wealthy merchant from Manchester, Samuel Grimshaw, built and founded the hall in about 1841. The Grimshaw family were resident here from then until 1930 when the last member of the family died. They were a wonderful asset to the valley, bringing secure employment and prosperity to its people. In addition they were very popular and respected by all who were privileged to have dealings with them, both in business and socially. They were enthusiastic travellers, introducing species of exotic plants from the world's more remote places to adorn their ornamental gardens within their grounds. Sadly this all ended in 1930 when Stockport Corporation purchased the estate and, a few years later, demolished the hall along with tenants' cottages and farms on the estate in order to construct Fernilee Reservoir, the first and larger one of the two in this valley.

At the rear of the ruined hall, about ³/₄ of a mile from the ruins of Castedge Farm and in the direction of Shooters Clough, the steep, winding track leads up to St Joseph's shrine. For visitors, this lovely shrine provides an opportunity for prayers and quiet reflection. This small round stone building has a sturdy oak door which, when opened, reveals a small altar with a picture of St Joseph holding the Baby Jesus. Just above this picture is a little marble slab with a Latin inscription in tribute to the saint. The family cemetery is also situated on the hillside, above the hall's ruins. It's a most poignant, atmospheric place.

After a most enjoyable and interesting ramble we went back to Errwood car park where our transport was waiting for us and returned to Buxton over the Long Hill Road (A5004). On our return journey we saw a view of the famous Bunsal Cob incline on the Goyt Valley section of the old Cromford & High Peak Railway. This section was closed in 1892 because the new link to Buxton via Stockport, Disley and Whaley Bridge was completed. Again the scenery here, as on all these routes, is breathtakingly beautiful with pleasant surprises along the way. Set in one of the stone walls adjoining Long Hill Rd, is a plaque commemorating the Grimshaw children's popular Spanish governess. Each time I saw it during one of our trips to Goyt Valley, a fresh-looking bunch of flowers had been placed upon it, giving this shrine a delightful finishing touch.

The "Grimshaw Graveyard, Errwood Hall".

St Joseph's Shrine.

Discovery Trails

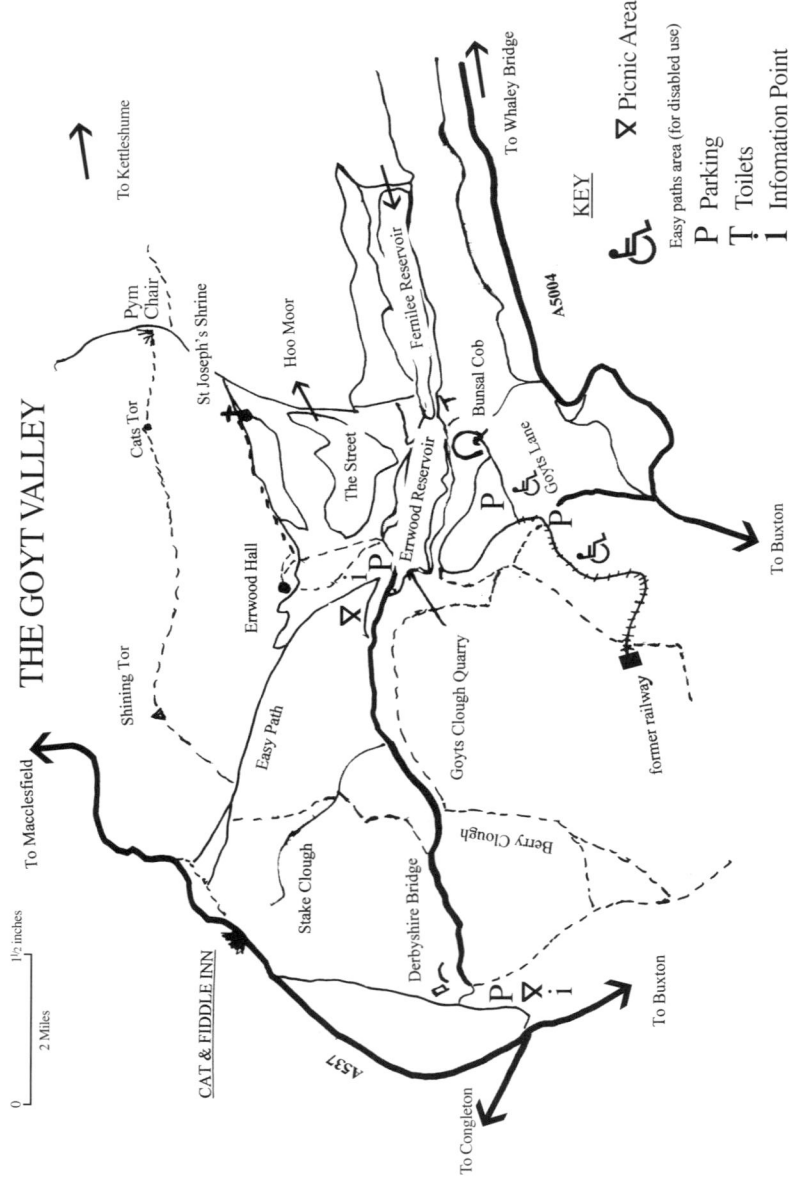

Along the towpath where bridges and banks have tales to tell

Disley to New Mills along Peak Forest Canal towpath.

Distance: Two and three quarter miles altogether. (Two and a half on this particular walk as I took a detour for a quarter of a mile towards Strines).

Public transport links: Buses: **199** Trent, Buxton-Stockport service, **361** Stagecoach, Stockport-Glossop service. By train: Manchester-Stockport route via New Mills Newtown.

Facilities: 2 pubs in Disley centre – Dandy Cock (their tasty snacks and full meals are super value for money) and the Ram's Head. The

Ram's Head has better disabled access and its spacious interior makes it easier for wheelchair customers to manoeuvre round. 2 large pubs in Strines, also with good sized car parks, adjacent to main B6101 road to Marple. **New Mills** - The Swan Hotel at Newtown and the Derbyshire Chippy, on the corner of Wirksmoor Rd and adjoining Albion Rd, off the main A6 Stockport-Buxton Rd.

Public toilets by Disley Rail Station yard.

Extra Information Note: If you wish to access Peak Forest Canal from Marple (or do the full walk along the towpath from Marple to New Mills) there are two main access points – the Marple one is via the footway on both sides of the A626 Station Rd by the bridge over the canal, a short distance from Rose Hill Rail Station. Famous Marple Aqueduct is close by. The Strines one is at Plucksbridge Rd, off the B6101 Strines Rd (to the right if approaching from Marple).

Public transport links: **By rail:** Manchester-New Mills service from New Mills Central Station. This train stops at Strines and Marple Rose Hill. **By bus: 358** Stagecoach service Glossop/Hayfield to Stockport via Strines and Marple.

Access for disabled people to the canal towpath

Strines Bridge 21 – Grid ref: SJ 965 870

Access located on Plucksbridge Rd, off the B6101 Strines Rd, between Marple and Strines. Care needed because of slight gradient and unevenness. Plucksbridge Rd is steep so it's best to drive up the road to the canal bridge. There is parking space opposite the access point to the towpath. The length of the towpath further on between bridges 22 and 23 is too narrow for wheelchair use.

Disley Bridge 27 – Grid Ref SJ 986 848

Access located on Lower Greenshall Lane which winds steeply downhill to the North (the left as approached from the centre of Disley) from the A6 Buxton Rd (landmark – new oriental restaurant). However, Lower Greenshall Lane is not wheelchair accessible so a car would be essential in order to drive down the steep, bumpy slope from the A6. Access itself is good with a smooth, packed earth surface. Track is wide so it's possible to park your car near the canal bridge for access to the towpath.

Newtown **Near Bridge 28** – Grid Ref: SJ 997 849

Access located on Victoria St, off the A6015 Albion Rd (to the right if approaching from the junction with the A6). Path from road to towpath is uneven in places but not much gradient to be negotiated and there is sufficient width.

Friday, 21st November, 2003

This was a most interesting and memorable ramble as, after taking part in the annual Children In Need Fundraising Day at the Dandy Cock, a small, cosy and friendly pub on Disley's main street, I took the downward path at the side of this hostelry, by its clear sign in the low stone wall – Hollinwood Rd. It was a lovely afternoon, cool in temperature but bright, clear and sunny – ideal for a country stroll in winter "far from the madding main road traffic". This last statement is somewhat inaccurate as two railway lines following two separate routes run close to the canal at various points as does the main A6 road from Stockport on route to Buxton. Nevertheless, the scenery along the towpath is very pretty.

It's a most pleasant walk down Hollinwood Rd and is about 7-8 minutes walk down to the canal. Along the way you see country cottages with ivy and rambler roses round their grey stone walls, brightly coloured heather and gorse plants adorn their window boxes. Soon the road splits into a junction. The path on the left-hand fork slopes uphill and is marked Hagg Bank Lane. Proceeding along this lane there are picturesque views to admire, of rolling wooded hills across to Strines and Marple, south to Lyme Park and east towards the moors above Mellor and New Mills. After a short while, by a hollow and clearing between the trees on the right-hand side, the swing bridge of Higgins Clough, the towpath and canal come into view.

I crossed this bridge onto the towpath by the remarkable, most scenic and interesting Peak Forest Canal. This canal is a special piece of industrial heritage as it was a complicated and ambitious feat of engineering for its time. It had to be built on two levels, the upper completed in 1796, the lower in 1800 and linked by a temporary tramway at Marple which was replaced in 1807 by the lock flight at the Grand Aqueduct. The lock flight has 16 locks – the second deepest in our country. Marple Grand Aqueduct was built in 1800, having taken seven years to complete, is 309 ft long (100 metres in metric) and looms up close on 100 ft above the river Goyt.

Returning to the present subject, I turned left at Higgins Clough Bridge and went along the towpath for about a quarter of a mile. It's a lovely stretch again with extensive views over Mellor Moor and Strines across to the Goyt Way and Marple. On this fine day, the bright sunshine contrasted vividly with sharp, dark shadows and reflections of the willow, oak and birch trees from the canal bank onto the semi-transparent, silver surface of the water. Subtle shades of green were dappled with shifting shadows of sunlight and shade. Two ducks, one a mallard, the other brown speckled, chased each other over the water in playful antics usually associated with spring time. One very old oak tree, nearly bare of leaves as befitting its wintry appearance, spread its branches out like weirdly-shaped, black pipe work – you can imagine this spot being a creepy place at night.

Two barges, one painted blue, the other in orange, floated lazily past the lock at Woodend Bridge, an hydraulic, lift-up bridge. From the towpath there are spectacular views over two local hills, Cobden Edge and Eaves Knoll and the dramatic sweep of Ollersett Moor. Woodend Bridge and the nearby farm of the same name are so called because there were two mills on this spot known as Little Woodend, which produced cloth to be patterned at Strines Printworks. These mills were demolished in the early years of the 20th century. Particularly along the upper level section of the Peak Forest Canal, industry and agriculture were very closely linked.

Further along the towpath I reached the stone bridge at the area known as Stanley Hall Wood. On the opposite side of the towpath is Disley golf course and very attractive it looked on this sunshiny day with its fine trees and landscaped, ornamental flower beds. Behind the golf course, across two fields, Stanley Hall, a black and white half-timbered manor house is situated. It's so old that it was described in a 13th century document as "of ancient tenure!" The original house was built in medieval times. Stanley Hall Wood proved to be an asset to Disley in an unexpected way. The seed nursery flower growers, Yates & Co of Manchester, used this wood as its growing area. Barges used to load up here with flowering plants and shrubs, then sail up the canal to Manchester to supply the local markets there. It was a thriving trade for many years. The Yates family lived nearby in a house called Little Woodend which was built around 262 years ago.

In the area close by the Strines-Marple stretch of this canal – in fact all sections where the old cotton mills were situated, there are many footpaths and basic, "rough and ready" roads which now provide pleasant, interesting country walks. These paths most likely originate from the days when people who lived in the countryside within the canal's vicinity, walked several miles to and from their place of employment which was usually one of the local cotton mills or the large printworks at Strines. Of course they had to do this in all weathers. Tough characters in those days!

From this spot I walked a short distance further on where yet again picturesque views across Strines predominate. Recently the old Strines Printworks has been sold to the housing development company to be converted into residential properties. Near the redundant printworks there were still a few small workshops manufacturing steel tubing and wiring coils for various uses in industry. Around two years ago their managements tried to negotiate with the local authority to persuade them to refuse planning permission for a proposed new housing development there. The local people were also opposed to the new housing development on this site and formed themselves into a protest group to fight the proposals and back up the small firms as well. Apparently there was a conflict of interests regarding this site as the local authority maintained that it was unsuitable for industry to continue in operation there. However this view ignored the fact that some kind of industry has always been carried on at this old printworks site. Firstly planning permission for the housing development was refused after appeal by the small firms on the site.

Next, a public inquiry was held and the building company's application for planning permission was refused again. However, a fair compromise was worked out whereby half the site has been allocated for the new housing development and the other half for the small firms to stay and carry on their work. Two of the smaller factories will just be moved and re-allocated to other parts of the site. This decision appears at first instance to be a sensible and balanced one but the local protest group are still dissatisfied with the outcome and hope to challenge it by taking legal action before too long. As a couple of the workshops on site use noisy machinery in the course of their manufacturing processes, the group understandably fear that the small firms plus present and future employment provision will be sacrificed in favour of the housing development (who'd want to buy a new home close to factories which needed to use noisy machinery regularly?) It will be interesting to discover what the final outcome of this controversial issue turns out to be.

To return to my afternoon ramble on this interesting canal section, I then retraced my steps along the towpath slowly back home to New Mills as it was too pleasant an afternoon to hurry back onto the next access bridge to the main road for the nearest bus stop. The canal looped round a long bend by Roach Hey Wood, noted for its pretty scenery and a gap in the trees gave a clear view of Waterside Mill, originally water powered, firstly being a cotton mill and later a paper mill. Over the 200 years of its life, its original building was greatly extended. Some of its oldest parts were demolished. It's now occupied by Kruger Manufacturing Company who produce tissues.

A relatively short distance onwards brought me once again back to Higgins Clough Bridge. The vicinity round this bridge was an important industrial section of this canal in the early 19th century. There used to be a wharf here, a tramway to the lime kilns dotted along the route up to and including Marple and a coal mine, the shaft of which is now buried under Hagg Bank Lane near Hagg Bank Farm. Acomical tale found in this area's local history records state that in the early 19th century the farm was isolated as the neighbouring houses had not then been built. One night the widow who lived there heard repeated sounds of knocking in the barn. Understandably frightened, she asked some local villagers for help. Their vivid imagination made them believe the devil was there and so they tried, unsuccessfully, to exorcise the evil spirit. A soothsayer or wise local woman told the widow that a neighbour had put a curse on her but the neighbour would shortly be dead and consequently the knocking would cease. This happened as predicted so fortunately the widow now had peace of mind. She never knew that the mine owner, on hearing about the noises which caused the widow anxiety and fear, had investigated and discovered that a miner was working directly underneath the barn and, co-incidentally, ordered him to stop, just at the time when the neighbour died!

After this bridge the stretch up to New Mills has less open country, is more urban and built up but nevertheless attractive. Between Higgins Clough Bridge and Dryhurst Bridge, the next bridge en route to New Mills so called after woodland of the same name below the towpath, there is a small footpath for use of boats moored on the offside and to provide access to Disley village centre. At this point called Higgins Clough there was severe flooding in the 1940's. Also at this spot is the attractive black and white painted cottage now called Watersedge formerly named Kiln Cottage because of its close proximity to the lime kilns, was so flooded out that it had to be temporarily abandoned. Again in 1973, history repeated itself when a terrible storm caused the canal to burst its banks once more. It flooded the valley below and poured like a mighty torrent into the River Goyt which was already full to its brim. As ill fortune would have it, this was just at the time when the canal was due to be re-opened after being restored from semi-dereliction. Since then both banks have been re-enforced with concrete to prevent any future breaching and disintegration of the canal. Watersedge has also been restored and now had a landscaped front garden with topiaried trees, two of them box-shaped, one like a pointed magician's hat and one like mini castle walls teased into plaited patterns. Swans build their nests along this stretch and mallard ducks are often seen here. Occasionally kingfishers have been spotted nearby.

The lime kilns close to Watersedge Cottage were there until the early part of the 20th century. They were owned by the farmer at Hagg

Bank Farm (close to the lane named after it). An old advert in the Manchester Mercury dated 1806, offered the collieries' farm and lime kilns for sale or lease by private contract and informed the commercially enlightened public of the day that "an active purchaser could expect to make a profit of at least £1,000 per year." The premier business opportunity of Napoleonic times. Just imagine what that extra income would provide for you some 200 years ago!

Remarkably, between Disley and New Mills, the narrow valley of the River Goyt accommodates the Peak Forest Canal, two main roads, the A6 (Stockport-Buxton) and the B6101 (Marple route), just below Higgins Clough, trains run through Disley Tunnel on the Manchester/Sheffield line and, on the southern side, runs the Manchester to Buxton line via New Mills Newtown. Disley Tunnel runs under the Hagg Bank area and was completed in 1902 for the Midland Railway Direct line. It's absolutely straight, 2 miles 346 yards long and its other exit is near where the former High Lane station used to be. This station was on the old Marple to Macclesfield line via Poynton which was axed by Dr Beeching in 1970 and is now the Middlewood Way, a superb local trail for ramblers and cyclists.

The next bridge I came to is Dryhurst Bridge, so called after a small wooded copse of the same name. By this stone bridge you can leave the towpath and canal to return to the main A6 road on to New Mills. The road over Dryhurst Bridge is named Red House Lane which derives its name from the White Lion pub, adjacent to the A6. This pub has been painted white for many years but was originally built of red brick so it was known locally as "the red house". Red House Lane was the old road from New Mills to Disley, predating both the A6 and the B6101. Modern traffic made this road redundant as a main one because its route into New Mills via Hague Bridge and Hague Fold was both narrow and steep. Even stagecoaches during the 18th and early 19th centuries had their work cut out to negotiate the hairpin bends en route. Much later on in the early 20th century, a local factory by the canal were having some long cylindrical boilers delivered from Lancashire, on using this narrow lane, discovered they were too big to be transported under the bridge so during weekend the road had to be dug out, the sewers moved and then the whole lot replaced after the boiler delivery so it's a wonder it lasted as long as it did as a main highway. Just beyond this bridge, on the opposite bank from the towpath, is the Bowater Factory complex.

Just before I reached Knathole Wood, on the towpath side, I saw a Canada goose. There's no mistaking the long, black neck and black patch with a white stripe in between on its forehead. These species are becoming increasingly common on our local canals and rivers. Going past Knathole Wood I noticed how attractive it looked in its rusty gold autumnal glory. It has rather steep slopes but there are some paths and ways into the wood from here. You have to be selective as again they tend to be steep. The wood stretches along the Goyt to Mouseley Bottom via the Goyt Way Trail (in addition to Peak Forest Canal towpath, Goyt Way Trail can be accessed by crossing the Millennium Bridge at the Torrs Riverside Park and by the footpath at New Mills Central Station approach). Mouseley Bottom was the original way into New Mills before the Industrial Revolution and the consequential building of new roads round here i.e. Albion Rd built in 1835 replaced the old road and linked up Newtown with the rest of New Mills.

At Newtown, opposite The Swan pub, is Overdale Rd. At the bottom end of this road, near the canal and high up a slope in a field, is the LNWR (London North Western Railway) cutting, a relic of the abandoned Disley to Hayfield railway. The reason for it not being completed was because there was already a railway planned which covered virtually the same route and which is now the Sett Valley Trail so understandably it was considered unnecessary to have two railways running side by side for the last two miles from New Mills to Hayfield. There is also an abandoned short stretch of the Peak Forest Canal around the bottom end of Overdale Rd area like a dugout basin still containing some water. The reason why this section of canal was never completed was that it would have been in the direct path of the railway line so it was sacrificed to the construction of the Stockport-Buxton line back in 1867.

As you come into New Mills along the canal towpath, there is also an end section of an embankment visible on the far side of the towpath, opposite Swizzels factory, another relic of this lost railway, testimony to the cutthroat competition by various rail companies to secure territory for commercial advantage in the rapidly expanding rail network of Victorian times.

After passing Knathole Wood, it wasn't long before I reached the Swizzels Sweet Factory. It smelled very tempting, its vicinity pleasantly warm – ideal on a winters' day walk. The canal winds under the bridge at Albion Rd, emerging at New Mills Marina, now a depot of Anglo Welsh Holiday Cruisers which has taken over the site of Victoria Wharf and mill warehouse. Close by, through a yard, is Redmoor Supplies, the local builders merchants and DIY specialists.

I emerged from the marina onto Victoria Street, turned right into Albion Rd and then back home after a most interesting and enjoyable walk.

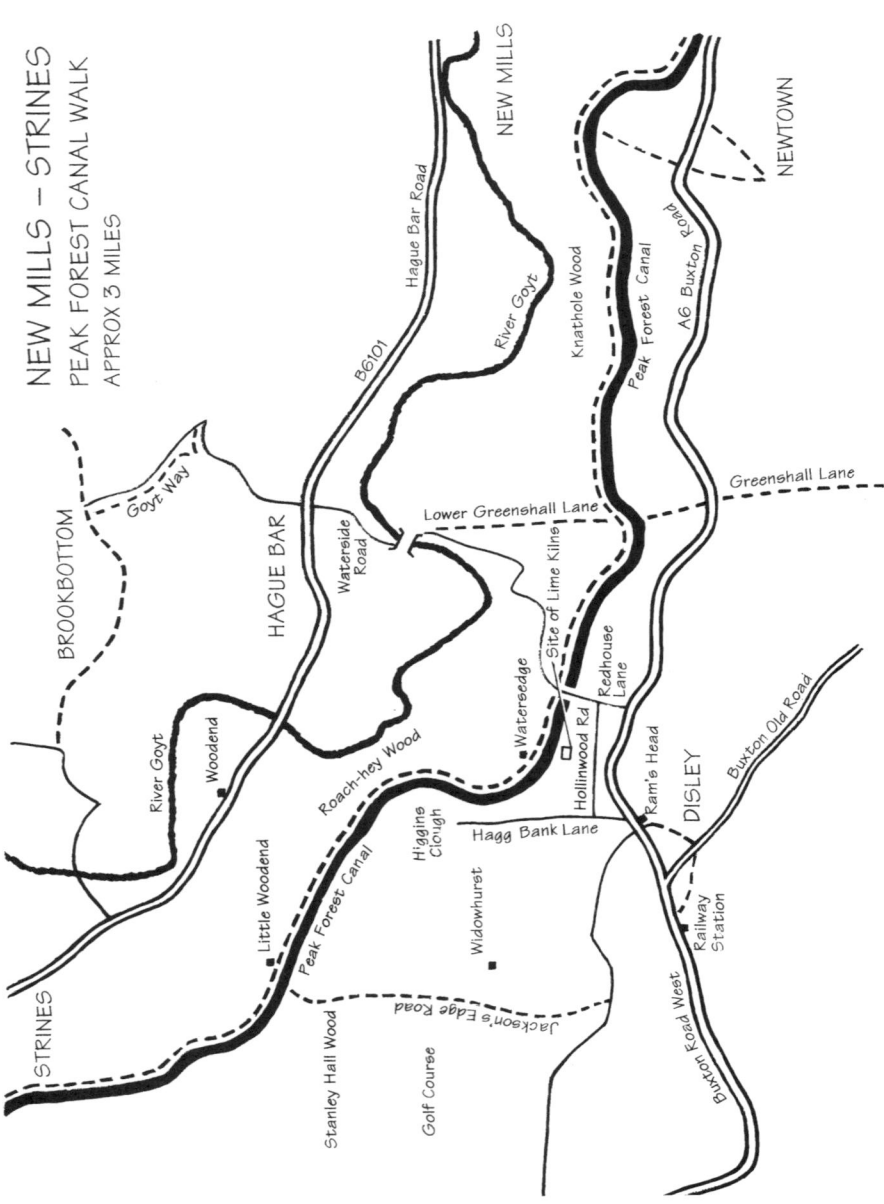

Hayfield Moorland Taster

By the River Sett, to Bowden Bridge and O'er the Tops.

Distance: Between two and a half and three miles altogether.

Facilities: Selection of pubs and cafés in Hayfield. The Royal Hotel, (disabled toilet–womens' only) The Bull's Head, The George, The Sportsman and Kinder Lodge are best for disabled access and facilities.

Public toilets at Hayfield Information Centre (next to bus station). Also at Hayfield Campsite on the right hand side of the access road leading through the wooden gates onto Edale Road. Disabled toilet included. The Kinder Trail path from the village centre runs via Church St and Valley Rd, then directly above the River Sett to the campsite. This path is suitable for wheelchair users, pushchairs, etc.

Public transport links: Bus Services. Stagecoach **358** from Stockport and **361** on Stockport-Hayfield-Glossop route, Peak Bus Network **61** Buxton-Glossop route and Bowers **355**. Last-named runs on weekdays only.

I was privileged to participate in this most interesting, scenic gem of a ramble, twice over, firstly on the final Tuesday of October, 2002 and on the last Friday in September, 2003. Both rambles were organised by the Peak Park Rangers. On both occasions, our party seemed fated to begin our ramble in chilly, wet and misty conditions. Nevertheless we intrepid walkers were living in hopes that the weather would improve at some point on route, preferably before lunchtime as we'd all been provided with packed lunches and cartons of fruit juice obviously to consume outdoors.

On the first walk we went up Church St to the spot known locally as "Top O' The Town" and from there, turning right on to Valley Rd, we followed the course of the River Sett towards Hayfield Campsite. This route is always a visual delight all the year round with the clear river sparkling in sunlight, creating a kaleidoscope of many shades, tumbling over weathered boulders and gritstones. On our autumnal rambles the colours were glorious with the trees and bracken along the river banks turning varied hues of yellow, golden brown and rusty orange, contrasting vividly with the bright green moss on the banks and in random spots on the grass by woodland. We spotted a grey heron on the river bank. It caught a small fish dexterously in its beak. As the Sett is a trout river, herons, kingfishers, swallows and swifts find a convenient source of extra food here so many nests are built along its banks.

On the other side of the river, just past the path leading up to the Sportsman Inn, a pleasant country pub perched on the side of a steep valley which winds above the Sett, is the stone railway embankment which was constructed to carry the railway up to Kinder Reservoir back in 1902. After a short distance we moved to the left through a stone "kissing gate" just the right width for wheelchairs. Our ranger pointed out that the railway, which transported materials and men to the site of Kinder Reservoir when its construction was underway, crossed the river at this point on a trestle bridge. One of the old stanchions low down by the wall in the opposite bank is visible here.

We were now walking along the track bed of the old railway. On the right is Hayfield Campsite which used to be owned by the Peak Park Authority but is now leased to the Caravan & Campers Association of Great Britain. It's a good site with a shop/information centre and hot showers in the toilet blocks. It occupies land known locally as Puddlefield (a somewhat inappropriate selling point especially to potential campers!) because of the clay that was dug here to line the reservoir dam. The right kind of clay was sought all over the country and even abroad but was eventually excavated right on the doorstep!

In the 17th century the field now occupied by the campsite was known as Cutler's Green. A door lintel carved N. W. 1617 is set in the stone wall on the river side. N W stands for Nicholas Wilkinson who had a workshop making cutlery here. In 1634 he was brought before Buxton Quarter Sessions accused of being a recusant which meant not attending the Anglican Church but instead a Roman Catholic or Nonconformist one – this was the time of religious intolerance. Present day Christians of the latter-named denominations must feel most thankful that they weren't around in those days!

Altogether this place certainly had a chequered history. Before the reservoir construction was started, Kinder Printworks stood here. Built in the mid-19th century, it was demolished in 1900 because of rampant financial difficulties. (probably competition from several rival print factories such as the Watford one at New Mills, Strines Printworks and others dotted around the locality rendered it unprofitable).

To return to the present: wheelchair users and people with prams and pushchairs can enjoy three pleasant walks back into Hayfield by passing the campsite shop and following the access road leading out through the wooden gates onto Edale Road. There are public toilets on the right. Firstly, though, they should see the plaque on the rock face of the quarry opposite which commemorates the famous Kinder Trespass which started from here back in 1932. Then turn left over the bridge and left again, returning to Hayfield along Kinder Road.

The second walk leads left over the bridge then right up Kinder Road for half a mile to reach Kinder Reservoir gates. Then retrace one's steps back into Hayfield, after admiring the sheepwash on the right side of the bridge, similar to the one at Ashford-in-the-Water. The third walk is straight along Edale Road, past Hayfield Fishing Club. Then the road bends to the right and on the opposite side are two benches, making this spot an ideal place for a picnic with a lovely view over the old stone packhorse bridge which spans the River Kinder just before joining the Sett. There are also waterfalls to admire further along Edale Road where the Sett crosses a stone bridge. Whichever spot is chosen, wheelchairs prams and pushchairs need to turn back on sighting the moorland paths here as these are too steep for safe access.

To return to my narrative: We then turned left on Kinder Road, over the bridge and onto Bowden Bridge Quarry, now used as a car park. On its face, we read the plaque commemorating the famous Kinder Mass Trespass in 1932. This act of defiance by ramblers entering the landowner's territory, the moors above Kinder Reservoir reserved by the local gentry for grouse shooting, for which the protesters were convicted and imprisoned, drew public attention to the issue of access to the open countryside for recreation beneficial to all, not just a privileged elite and brought about new legislation granting universal access to the countryside. National Parks in areas of outstanding natural beauty were established throughout our land, the Peak District National Park being the first one back in the early 1950's.

From the quarry, following the left-hand side of the river we then proceeded to Bowden Bridge, a lovely wooded spot (but distinctly unlovely in the rain and mist on our second ramble up here) and then continued, still keeping to the left to the sheepwash at Booth Bridge which has a plaque fixed to it containing the information that Hayfield Civic Trust are doing restoration work on this feature. Sheep farming was the most suitable kind of agricultural activity for this moorland area, hence the number of hill farms nearby and, consequently, the need for the sheepwash. The farmers or their family members, in fact, whoever did the routine work at the wash was paid one whole penny at the local market for each cleaned fleece so the sheepwash would have been well used for many centuries.

We then walked up to Booth Farm, the farmhouse dating from the 18th century – hence the carved inscription on its front. You almost go through the farmyard to join another stony moorland track which is a steady ascent, up to a gate and along a ridge from which you can see an impressive view of Kinderscout's western flank. We stopped on grass verges close to the path to eat our packed lunches and drink our liquid refreshment. This was not the uncomfortable experience we expected as, by then, the weather started to brighten up and the rain ceased although on both occasions it was cold for the time of year.

From the top moorland path we gradually descended and the track became a smoother, properly surfaced path. As with most of its length, this route is a wonderful one for seeing panoramic views with purple heather, bracken and gorse in colourful clumps on the moors and woodland plantations dotted around on various stretches. On route we came across another farmhouse dating from the early 19th century. Both farms looked like an ideal setting for filming "Wuthering Heights" or more appropriately now, its sequel, "Return to Wuthering Heights" by Nicola Paige in which the famous novel was extended to move on with the story of the next two generations of the two feuding families. In fact our ranger friend said that there was a dispute between two local farming families here in these hills except that, fortunately, it did not last as long as the one in Emily Bronte's novel.

Just past the farm and beyond another gate along the downward path, members of our party and I spotted several black sheep and some wild ponies in the fields to our right. These animals did not seem at all perturbed at us taking photos of them but obviously they must be used to ramblers frequenting this area. Keeping straight on down the path we eventually reached a bridge where the junction with Bowden Bridge Quarry car park and the campsite is situated. We turned right, onto the campsite access road, followed this road past the rangers' post and downstream on to Valley Road. We passed the recreation ground at Valley Road on the right and finally re-entered the village at Top O'The Town junction of Valley Rd, Highgate Road and Church Street.

Altogether adventure, historical interest, wildlife and scenery all combined to make this ramble an exciting package, notwithstanding changeable, chilly weather.

Discovery Trails

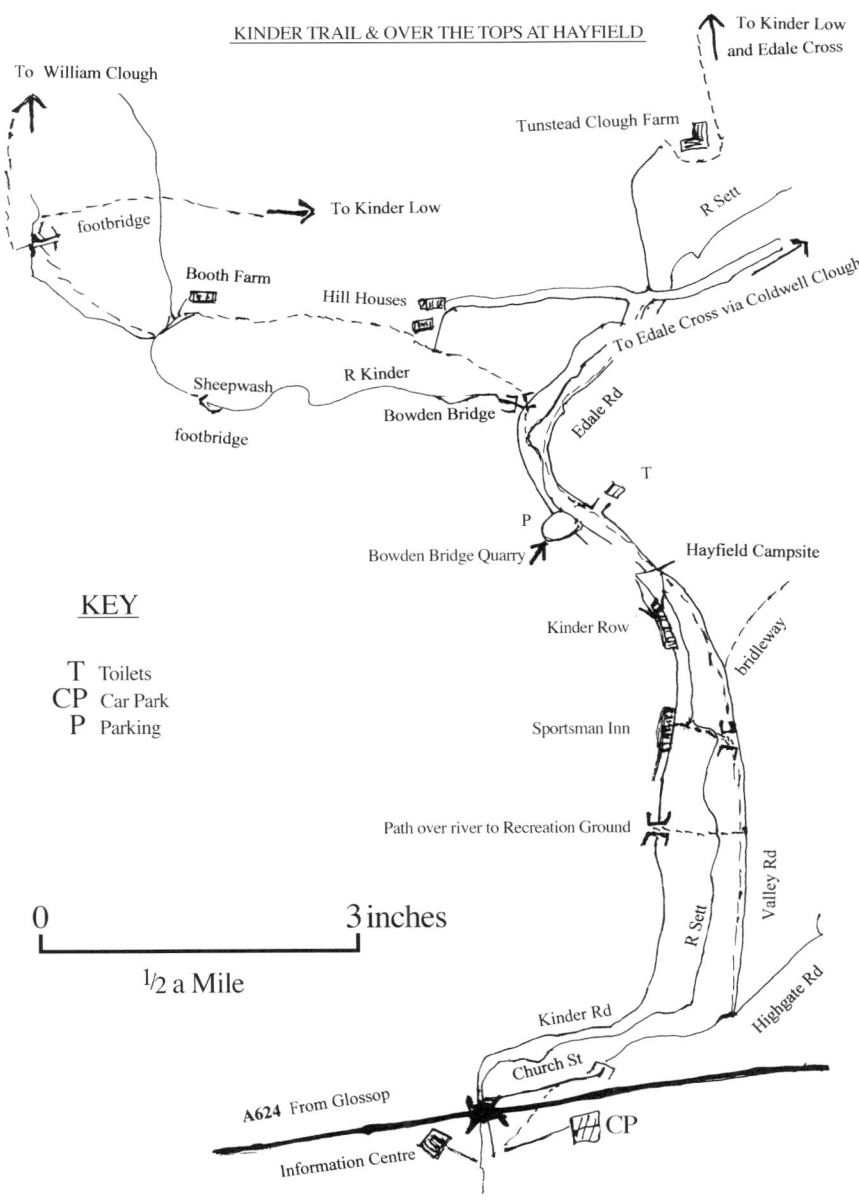

Two Inns, a Canal, a former Railway now a country trail, a Transformed Coal Mine Site –altogether a best value ramble!

Distance: One and a half miles each way

Facilities: Refreshments: High Lane - Dog & Partridge, Bull's Head, Reflections Café' (booking advisable) Higher Poynton - Boar's Head, Coffee Tavern, The Trading Post at main Higher Poynton Marina Car Park has a canal shop and also serves hot and cold drinks, crisps, chocolate biscuits, ices, etc.

Pubs with facilities for Disabled People: Red Lion Inn, Dog & Partridge, Bull's Head all at High Lane. Lyme View Café' at Wood Lane East, Adlington (next village close to the canal after Higher Poynton and towards Bollington).

Disabled Facilities: Easy wheelchair access point to canal from car park at The Trading Post, Higher Poynton Marina. Wheelchair access with assistance onto canal towpath and the Middlewood Way Trail via corner of Shrigley Rd North. Various other access points for wheelchairs - assisted access at Jackson Brickworks car park close to Middlewood Way, on Wood Lane by café and bridleway near Poynton Coppice, assisted access at footpath close to Poynton Coppice.

Toilets & Information Point: Nelson Pit Visitor Centre.

Public transport links: 199 Trent bus runs between Stockport & Buxton via New Mills Newtown, **361** Stagecoach Stockport-Glossop service. Also **392** and **393** Arriva Northwest Stockport-Macclesfield service via Bollington, Adlington and Poynton (stop by church).

My younger daughter, Emily, and I were fortunate twice over in taking the opportunity to join this most scenic and interesting towpath walk by Macclesfield Canal. Our first walk was on the last Tuesday in February and again on Easter Monday 12th April 2004. On both occasions this proved to be a discovery trail embracing industry of the past and the natural world in our own time.

We started our ramble from The Bull's Head pub at High Lane, adjacent to the A6 Stockport to Buxton road. The Bull's Head used to be very much a miner's pub used by workers from the coal mines dotted around Poynton. Directly en route was Nelson Pit at Higher Poynton which is now a visitor centre situated just round the left-hand corner from the end of this stretch of the towpath. The field behind the Bull's Head used to be a site of bare knuckle fights back in the 1820's between the miners and the navvies who were constructing the canal. When proceeding along the towpath it's not long before you come across evidence of commercial activity from the 19th and 20th centuries right up to the 1960's. In the sturdy, well built bridges, notice the grooves in them made by ropes causing friction from the towing horses, crossing over the bridges where the towpath changed sides, with their cargoes in the boats, sometimes heavy goods such as tubs of coal. Beer used to be delivered to this pub in barrels through a tunnel which no longer exists. To this day, local historians and industrial archaeologists alike are baffled as to exactly where it ran from. Another interesting fact about the history of the Bull's Head – it used to be the inn used by working class travellers or indeed anyone of more limited financial means. The posh, wealthy people used to stay at the Ram's Head or the Dandy Cock in Disley. This is probably why Disley has a classy somewhat aristocratic image locally.

The towpath is just below the pub, accessed by a flight of sturdy stone steps. At this point on the towpath, it's a most romantic spot in appearance with weeping willows, silver birch and topiaried trees, creating a picture of surrealistic deep green shapes on the light brown/old gold surface of the water. The small café on the opposite bank is most aptly named Reflections. A short distance from the eateries, two bright red barges with highly polished gold livery came into view. These barges appear to be permanently moored there as we saw them at this same spot on our earlier ramble down here. A short distance further along the towpath is a notice publicising interesting facts about High Lane village. This village used to be on the main route to Stockport and Manchester before Roman times – therefore an ancient highway stop. (must have been a somewhat long winded journey to either place in those days!) Also mentioned on the notice is the information that there used to be a cotton mill at Andrew Lane. This narrow lane with a definite country feel to it, can easily be reached by an entrance to the canal at the opposite side of the A6, directly opposite the Bull's Head. The wharf which was connected to this mill was on the offside of the canal near Marple.

We continued along the towpath, admiring the lovely views out over the Cheshire Plain and noting the turnings to the right of this path. The first turning is marked by a large notice which reads Ladybrook Valley/Middlewood for rail station. By this spot is a public footpath which winds through the woods down to this quiet little country station, situated half a mile west of the canal, where trains run hourly to Stockport and Buxton. It's an odd place for a railway station, being so remote that there's no road access. Your only option is to use the woodland path by the Ladybrook Valley sign. This path runs adjacent to the Stockport-Buxton rail line-opened in 1857. This line has one of the steepest gradients in our national rail system.

There's another interesting surprise in store just past Middlewood Station. If you turn left here and keep to the left-hand track, walk on for about 5 minutes then turn left again for Jackson Brickworks Conservation Site, signposted here. The brickworks closed in 1979 and was derelict until Macclesfield Borough Council took over the site in 1996 and developed it into a nature conservation area. It's now a habitat for great crested newts and water voles in ponds that used to be the old clay pits. After industry had moved out, the local wildlife has truly moved in. (as the sitting or swimming tenants, rent free!) There's also wetlands, grassland, willow, birch and hawthorn trees which, in turn, attract a variety of birds including long-tailed tits, blue tits, black caps, bullfinches, garden warblers and kingfishers.

Ladybrook Valley has an interesting trail along it which stretches all the way to Abney Hall at Cheadle, where it meets up with the River Mersey. This trail winds close to Bramhall Park, an old Elizabethan black and white half-timbered manor house on what is a pretty countryside route, one of the many public footpaths leading off the canal and the Middlewood Way close by, an extensive network, tempting many a more adventurous rambler as well as shorter routes providing equally pleasant country walks. Look out for large pot-holes and remains of embankments, straight tracks to and from the pits all testimony to the area's industrial past, especially sites of coalmines and railways.

For budding botanists, many wild flowers are in abundance along these trails. In fact, on all these walks from different starting points on the canal and Middlewood Way routes from High Lane to Higher Poynton have stretches where wild flowers form a riot of colour throughout spring, summer and well into "reet back end" otherwise known as October. On rambles during October in the late 1990's with the Peak Park Rangers (based in Bakewell), my fellow ramblers and I came across species of wild flowers, around Millersdale in the Wormhill/Buxton area and also Macclesfield Forest, that should have died off in September so this is one bonus to our advantage from the milder climatic changes in recent years.

The second right-hand turning on the towpath is marked by a public footpath sign for Middlewood Way. On our first walk down here, approximately 1 year and 2 months ago, by this sign, we went down some stone steps and on to a dead straight path a several feet below the canal level, in a deep cutting with a raised section in the middle of the track – obvious remains of a railway. In fact the Middlewood Way which runs close to this canal, stretches for 11 miles from Marple to Macclesfield via Poynton and was the former railway covering this route. It carried stone from the quarries at Kerridge and cotton from the Bollington mills. This railway closed in 1970 as, despite being a success as a passenger railway especially before the growth of universal car ownership, the goods transportation side of its business always struggled to keep in profit. It was restored for recreation with a new identity as the Middlewood Way – a most encouraging regeneration success story.

Going straight on towards the Constellation Marina and Nelson Pit Visitor Centre, the Middlewood Way here is wooded and teems with wild flowers from springtime through to mid-autumn. It's a bit like going through a woodland tunnel with a canopy of branches of its taller trees meeting overhead, giving this section of the way a fairy tale feel.

Alternatively, you can continue along the towpath and arrive at the marina and visitor centre just the same. This was what we did on our second walk to the centre. Either way, you reach the arm of the canal at Higher Poynton and here, where both routes run close together, is the colourful marina. Each barge has its individual mooring clearly marked and, even when we hurried along through a sudden shower and had some fifteen minutes of overcast weather, it was uplifting to see the brightly painted and illustrated barges contrasting all the more vividly against a background of subdued light.

The upper levels of both the Macclesfield and Peak Forest canals provide over 23 miles of lock-free cruising so, in consequence, these lengths are very popular with weekend cruisers – hence a high number of barges proliferate here in fine weather.

When we reached the marina, being more knowledgeable about this vicinity on our second walk, we were also close to Brownhills Bridge, one of the flat-topped bridges, designed like this because of subsidence caused by extensive coal mining so they were easily dismantled and raised where necessary. The playing field alongside Brownhills Bridge was judged to be almost level with the canal when the latter was constructed but subsidence caused there to be a 4 metre drop! For narrowboat enthusiasts mooring is ideal here. There's a wide choice of walks, facilities and things to discover as you emerge from the towpath at Higher Poynton. At this spot a network of signposts clearly indicate your options.

The canal mooring area is known as Lord Vernon's Wharf, built by the 19th century local entrepreneur cum landowner to load boats with coal from this pit for distribution and supply round the various textile mills and quarries in the area. In much later times a local character, Edith Burgess, who resided permanently on her narrowboat "Edward" moored just outside the wharf, developed the boating business here. If boaters or walkers flouted the rules she imposed they were in for a severe reprimand from this sharp-tongued individual. However, to regular boaters and walkers who enjoyed the recreation the canal and its vicinity had to offer them, she was a generous spirited person who protected the canal for the benefit of all users. A memorial seat is now here; placed in recognition of her valuable contribution to the conservation of the canal and its area.

The visitor centre and its car park was the site of a coal mine called Nelson Pit – hence the visitor centre's name. The visitor centre, although small, contains an interesting exhibition about the history of the canal, railway and connecting industries, information leaflets about the many walks and forthcoming social events which the local rangers organise to help visitors make the most of their time spent in this interesting scenic part of North East Cheshire. There's also "hands-on" items with fun quizzes for children and teenagers to encourage them to develop an interest in countryside conservation. Altogether well worth a visit.

Looking down the road from the centre, directly ahead, by the junction at the Boars Head pub, is Anson Road. Walk a few yards along this road, past the treatment works and the Anson Museum is sign-posted which you soon reach. This museum houses a vintage collection of oil and gas engines used in the mines and an exhibition depicting the local coal mining industry in its heyday. It's open from May to October on Sundays 11.am to 4.30 pm. Admission is free.

By the junction of Anson Rd, Green Lane and Shrigley Rd North and opposite the bus stop for Stockport and Manchester, are the two popular eateries, the Boars Head and the Coffee Tavern. The original Boars Head was demolished in 1906 and replaced by the present, larger pub of the same name. It has a varied menu and, as with most catering establishments nowadays, large print ones are available for people with visual disabilities. Next door to the Boars Head is the Coffee Tavern which has a more interesting history. In the early 1870's, Lord Vernon, who owned the Poynton Pits, was concerned about his miners squandering their wages on intoxicating liquor in the local pubs so the Coffee Tavern was erected in 1876 as a 'temperance tavern' serving coffees and teas instead of alcoholic drinks. It had a function room for special occasions and a Sunday School. This pleasant café' was finally granted a licence to sell alcohol in 1998, 122 years after its opening! The Coffee Tavern also has a delightful tea garden at its back end with flower beds, trees providing shade from overly hot and dazzling summer sun, a topiary tunnel and a mini playground for younger children. Looking at this pretty garden, it's hard to believe that pigs once grazed here, providing a plentiful supply of bacon which was stored in the cellar, probably where the toilets are now, judging by the layout of the ancillary room space round the back. The local community certainly got their moneys' worth out of this place!

To return to my narrative about Nelson Pit Visitor Centre: Several walks from this visitor centre's car park include a signpost indicating that if you turn to the right at the rear of the car park, the track leads along a public footpath network to Lyme Park, Disley, the famous National Trust historic mansion, surrounded by beautiful gardens and a large deer park. The hall and park were used by BBC TV as part of their film set for their adaptation of Jane Austen's classic novel "Pride and Prejudice". Tel No for opening times is 01663 762023. This walk is about 1 $3/4$ miles.

There's another good one to Poynton Coppice, an ancient woodland to the south of Higher Poynton, towards Bollington – turn right at the visitor centre car park, follow the signpost to Coppice Road and a short footpath from there leads you into the wood. It's about 3 miles walk from the visitor centre. In the wood, bluebells, wood anemone, yellow archangel, common spotted orchid and wild garlic grow in plentiful clumps. The wood warbler, pied fly catcher and orange tipped butterfly are occasional visitors here. On route, close to the canal side, chiff-chaff and red wing are birds to spot during spring, summer and early autumn.

After a most interesting time at Higher Poynton we returned on the first occasion via a small housing estate to the right of the Middlewood Way railway bridge, keeping to the right until reaching and passing through a wooded gimmel, bringing us back onto the canal towpath towards the Ladybrook Valley sign and hence onto

High Lane. On the second occasion we returned all the way along the towpath to High Lane and were treated to more sights of colourful barges coasting lazily along shiny brown water tinged with deep green and some mallard ducks and Canada geese, squawking, sun bathing and swimming, happy to be alive in springtime.

Discovery Trails

HIGH LANE TO HIGHER POYNTON - VIA CANAL & MIDDLEWOOD WAY

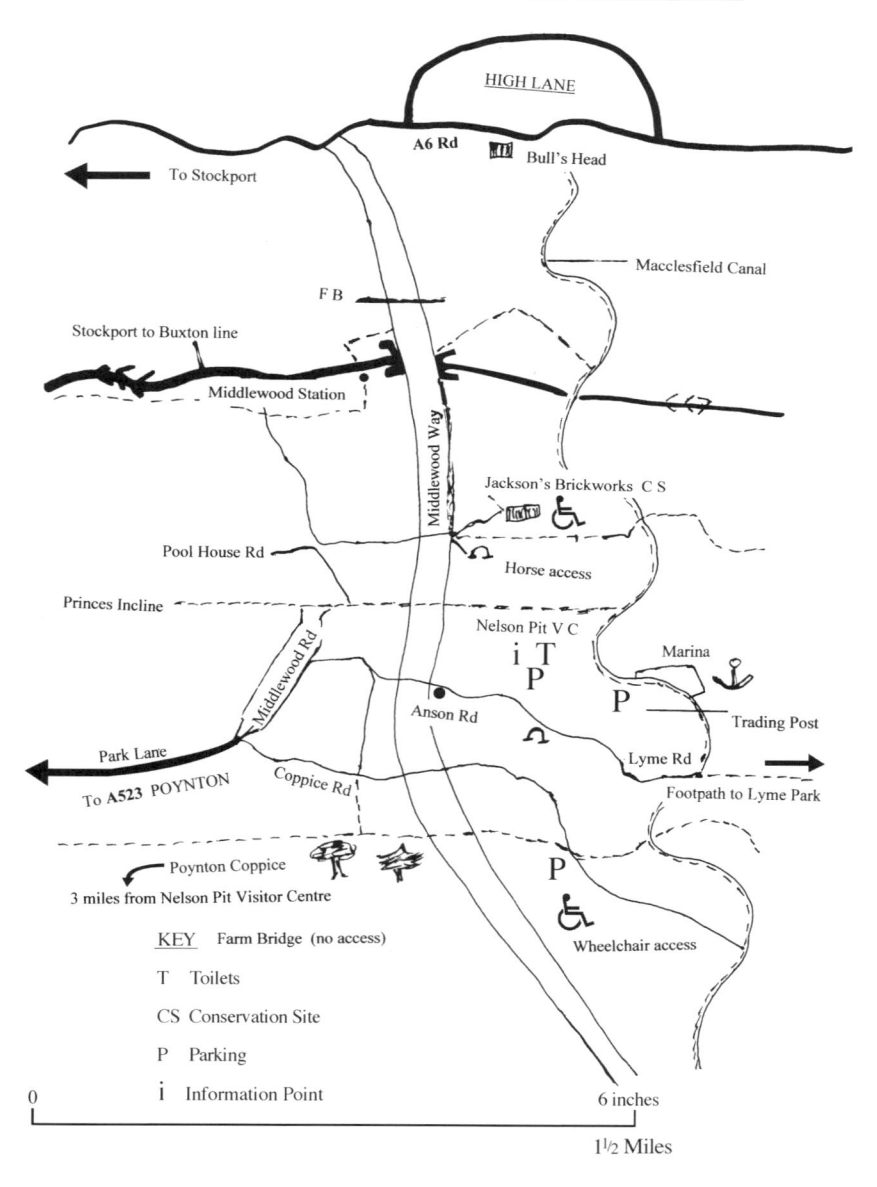

HIGH LANE

A6 Rd — Bull's Head

To Stockport

Macclesfield Canal

F B

Stockport to Buxton line

Middlewood Station

Middlewood Way

Jackson's Brickworks C S

Pool House Rd

Horse access

Princes Incline

Middlewood Rd

Nelson Pit V C

Marina

i T
   P

Anson Rd

P

Trading Post

Park Lane

Lyme Rd

To A523 POYNTON

Coppice Rd

Footpath to Lyme Park

P

Poynton Coppice
3 miles from Nelson Pit Visitor Centre

Wheelchair access

KEY   Farm Bridge (no access)
T   Toilets
CS   Conservation Site
P   Parking
i   Information Point

0 ———————————————— 6 inches

1½ Miles

46

Lose, Hope or Win

Trails around Hope including Losehill Hall area.

Facilities: Old Hall Inn and Woodroffe Arms Hotel in Hope; also cafes in main street. Parking at top of Pindale Rd, off A6187 Rd and opposite Hope Primary School. Visitor's car park at Losehill Hall, 2 miles from the village and along the same road in the Castleton direction.

Cafés and pubs in Hope which are most suitable for use by disabled people:
The Old Hall Inn (Market Place) Savoire Faire (The Courtyard) The Poachers (Castleton Rd) The Peak Inn (How Lane)

In Castleton the three most disabled friendly eateries are The Bull's Head, The Castle, Cryer House and The Stables.

At Castleton, there are refreshments available at cafes in the main street and at Ye Olde Nag's Head (former 17th century coaching house) also in village centre. Public toilets including disabled ones are in Castleton's main car park close to the village centre.

Public transport links: Manchester-Sheffield Hope Valley line - regular train service on weekdays and at weekends.

Bus services 173 Hulleys Bakewell-Castleton: **272** & **274** First South Yorkshire Sheffield-Castleton: **279** Stagecoach East Midlands Chesterfield-Castleton (Sundays & Bank Holiday Mondays only) **373** Speedwell Manchester-Castleton (Spring/Summer until late October weekends & Bank Holiday Mondays only) **202** TM Travel

Mansfield-Castleton (Spring/Summer until late October Sundays & Bank Holiday Mondays only.

On 3rd February, 2004 as the publicity officer of the newly formed Countryside Access Group, I accompanied the other members on a footpath research project. Countryside Access meet at Hope Clinic usually once a month to plan campaigns to raise awareness of the need for easier, more convenient access for disabled people to our beautiful countryside. We also liaise with the various relevant authorities who hopefully will offer us some practical support to achieve this most worthwhile aim.

Footpaths are usually taken for granted but it's very important that combined community effort involving the local authority, the Peak National Park Authority, (if in the Peak Park area – if not, sometimes the National Trust, British Waterways, English Heritage, etc) rangers and voluntary conservation groups all play their part in maintaining them. It means preserving a delicate balance between unrestricted access, observance of the countryside code and essential maintenance whereby routes used by ramblers, cyclists, horse riders and/or motorists have to be temporarily diverted for the work to be done without undue delay whilst also taking weather conditions into consideration.

Our research trip was interesting and enjoyable despite wet, cold weather. Eventually the sun did manage to struggle through grey woolly textured clouds for a few minutes and contrasted like gold and silver borders on weirdly shaped dust blobs.

On this occasion we surveyed the condition of the path leading from the left of the exit at Losehill Hall Study Centre car park down to Spring

House Farm which is adjacent to the main A6187 Hope Valley road. The Study Centre, which takes its name from a local hill mentioned later on in this chapter, provides courses in countryside management and conservation and holidays with emphasis on outdoor pursuits. We also surveyed hedges, checking for sharp, overhanging branches and twigs which would present a hazard for blind and partially-sighted walkers. The path's width was also measured to assess wheelchair access.

We measured the surface of the path where it was uneven and counted ruts which, on this wet, wintry day were water-logged, creating inevitable muddy puddles. The section near the hall and the one at the other end by Spring House Farm were properly tarmaced because they provide access for the study centre staff and the farmer and his family. Therefore our conclusion was that the middle section of this path was the part which needed the most attention. The surface could be considerably improved here at relatively minor expense.

The ranger who accompanied us on this useful countryside "detection" project explained that obviously locations such as this one don't have the same number of visitor facilities as you find in built-up areas or major tourist attractions. The criterion for deciding what facilities to include on country walks depends on the following considerations:

A. whether the area's ecology would be damaged by too many urban type facilities particularly wild-life habitats being disturbed;

B. whether the expense of including and maintaining facilities such as public toilets, refreshment kiosks, indoor information displays, etc would be worthwhile if, in more extensively remote, wilder locations they would only be used for around half the year and so would be of rather limited benefit to the public.

C. whether some disabled facilities might prevent or severely limit others from enjoying walks in that particular location i.e. natural unusual rock formations "carved up" to provide levelled paths for wheelchairs – some wild, beautiful places may have their visual delights reduced and choice of more challenging walks may be lost. As with many aspects of life, it's a matter of finding and maintaining a reasonable balance, having weighed up all the factors involved.

There are many paths around Losehill Hall, leading "over the tops" i.e. from Spring House Farm up to Losehill Pike round to the ridge of Back Tor and crags, then to Hollins Cross and on the downhill track to Castleton, other more gentle walks by streams and meadows where panoramic views over Hope Valley are an added bonus. Sometimes these walks can involve negotiating stiles and hilly terrain on some routes more than others.

If in doubt as to the suitability of any walk you have in mind, your local "Walks for Health" scheme often advertised by the local press, volunteer, community and heritage centres, etc is the best organisation to contact for friendly, helpful advice. The walks are organised by your local ranger service or your local branch of the National Trust and are usually divided into these categories:

1. **Wheels & Walks** – on paths suitable for wheelchairs being wide enough and with level surfaces.
2. **Easy** – 2-3 miles on relatively flat terrain, a couple of stiles,

"kissing gates" or gentle slopes at the most.
3. **Moderate** – between 3 and a half - 4 miles, some slopes, inclines and stiles, some rough paths but generally manageable for anyone who's reasonably fit.

We soon reached Spring House Farm so named because of the pretty, natural and clear stream which runs from the garden and under the road, emerging at a tree by a hollow opposite the farm. There is a path leading uphill on the far side of the farmhouse. A signpost close by, points in the direction of the uphill path and reads "Losehill". The famous local hill and Study Centre named after it both acquired their name from an ancient territorial dispute between two Iron Age tribes who lived to the left and right of the River Noe. In those times a battle took place called the Battle of the River Noe as that was where the disputed land was situated. The tribe in the settlement to the left of the river lost the battle so the hill on their side became Losehill and the hill to the right of the river became Win Hill as the other tribe won.

This uphill path takes you to the summit of Losehill which is 476 ft above sea level and, from this spot, dramatic, panoramic views of wild moorland, limestone ridges, deep gorges and lush river valleys can be admired.

Whilst waiting for our min-bus back into Hope we all had a little time to reflect on our small but nevertheless important research project. This short reconnaissance walk served as a reminder to me of the sterling work, often unrecognised, carried out by the friendly, helpful ranger service, to promote education, conservation, appreciation and respect for our countryside.

Discovery Trails

CASTLETON TRACK VIA BACK TOOR & LOSEHILL PIKE

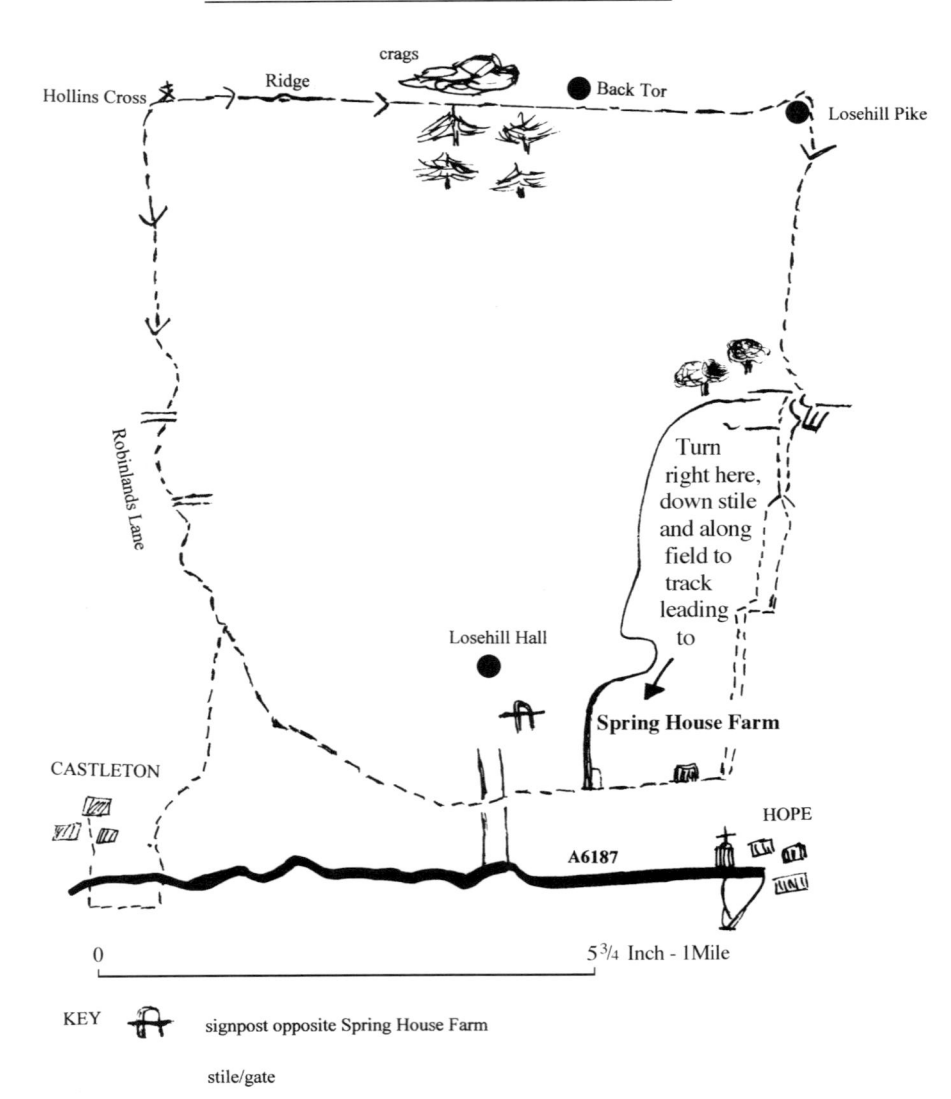

Hollins Cross — Ridge — crags — Back Tor — Losehill Pike

Robinlands Lane

Turn right here, down stile and along field to track leading to **Spring House Farm**

Losehill Hall

CASTLETON

A6187

HOPE

0 — 5 3/4 Inch - 1Mile

KEY — signpost opposite Spring House Farm

stile/gate

52

The Rosehill-Wyevale Experience

Distance: About 3 miles each way

Facilities: At Rosehill Rail Station - car park, toilets, ramp, access to and from platforms. Railway Hotel close by for refreshments. Also refreshments en route at Fish Bar (takeaway) and other cafes dotted round Marple centre. At the other end of this walk – Hare & Hounds pub, Wyevale Garden Centre has car park, café, toilets. Both these last named facilities are on Dooley Lane.

Public transport links: Stagecoach bus **358** Hayfield-Stockport, **394** Glossop-Hazel Grove (no service on Sundays & Bank Holiday Mondays), **X67** TM Travel Manchester-Chesterfield. By rail: Manchester-New Mills-Sheffield line via New Mills Central Station.

Important Note: I would **not** recommend this walk after a prolonged spell of wet weather or in winter/early spring after heavy rain or snow as it can be very muddy and slippery along the path by the River Goyt.

This walk is also unsuitable for people with mobility problems as the paths on the last section of this route are rather steep. There are other short walks around Marple which are relatively flat. Leaflets and guidance about them may be obtained from Marple Library in the Memorial Park or the Post Office in the main street.

One final point: If you wish to finish your walk by returning to Rosehill Station instead of going home from Wyevale Garden Centre, just retrace your steps back uphill, passing Marple Dale Hall School playing fields. You'll see the headstone and stone collection marking the site of old Marple Hall. When on Stockport Rd, turn left for Rosehill Station car park. This will add a mile extra to your walk.

On the 2nd week of March 2004, I set out from Rosehill Rail Station to Wyevale Garden Centre via the area known as Marple Dale and the public footpath along the banks of the Goyt. This proved to be an interesting walk with very pretty scenery along the way. I turned to the right just outside Rosehill Station and onto Stockport Road. This rather suburban route has nevertheless some most interesting features connected with the great feats of engineering, construction and trade developments during the Industrial Revolution. On route, directly across on the left-hand side of the road, I had a clear view of the famous Marple Aqueduct, an impressive stone structure with three lofty arches spanning the River Goyt. Completed in 1801, it took seven years to build. Journalists of the day commented that it was regarded as a truly great achievement in construction and engineering; the western world's equivalent of the Great Wall of China.

During this walk through to the tail end of the village centre, I enjoyed having a friendly, local lady as company up to parting near the Fish Bar adjoining the main B6101 road to Stockport. On route we passed the entrance to the Peak Forest Canal at the start of the stretch leading to Romiley. Here wheelchair access is possible with care from the footway on both sides of the A626 on Station Rd by its canal bridge. The lady kindly gave me directions to Bowden Lane, a slightly shorter route down to Dale Rd and the Goyt riverside track. I turned right at the next turning after what was then the Jolly Sailor pub (the building has now been converted into retirement apartments) onto

Bowden Lane, walked straight down to its bottom end which, at this point joins onto Dale Rd which, in turn, leads down to the river.

On the left-hand side of this attractive country road with its extensive woodland and river valley views is a side road prominently marked "The Turnpike" which was most probably a link on the old turnpike route in the days when the Turnpike Trusts collected tolls from road users to pay for their upkeep. In the early days of the Industrial Revolution these were virtually the only properly maintained roads so mill owners were keen to support the building of new ones leading directly to their mills. Sometimes there were disputes between mill owners about proposed local routes so even powerful, enterprising businessmen notably Samuel Oldknow, the cotton and muslin industry's leading entrepreneur in this area did not always have their wishes granted. When the Marple to New Mills turnpike road was being planned, Oldknow wanted the route to run from the street opposite his namesake road, in those days known as Rock Rd, through to his Mellor Mills, continuing on to the Roman Lake area, then to Strines and Brook Bottom, finally into New Mills. However, the higher ground route up the side of the Goyt river valley was selected instead. This is now the B6101, the way to Stockport via Strines and Marple, the route along which the 358 Stagecoach bus runs. I wonder if any of us can imagine what this road looked like when it was a turnpike one, just over 210 years ago? No doubt modern business executives would welcome the chance to enter a time walk and de-stress during an early 19th century rush hour!

To continue with the walk: After about 10 minutes' walk down Dale Rd, it narrows and slopes downhill, passing Marple Dale Hall Nursing

Home on the left. I proceeded along the wide track down into the valley. On its right-hand side, the ground falls away at a steep angle through the trees to the River Goyt. On reaching the bottom of the hill, I passed the Manchester Canoe Club building with the river accordingly marked off with practice areas. Hidden by trees and high up along the hillside, on the river's opposite side, runs the Peak Forest Canal.

I passed three farms along the track – Marple Dale, Middle Dale and Lower Dale. Up to Lower Dale Farm, the river banks are heavily filled with vegetation including willow, hawthorn and sycamore trees. Ferns, chickweed, ragged robin and, in later spring and summer, wood sorrel, bluebells, foxgloves and rosebay willow herb all grow profusely here. The damp weather conditions consisting of light showers and sunny periods and wet track, slippery with mud in places, proved to be a nuisance, turning my ramble almost into an assault course (felt I'd qualify for joining a challenging session at the local outdoor pursuits centre at Whaley Bridge!) I observed, when finally pausing for a breather, that changeable, wet weather in the countryside, especially in spring and autumn, combined with sporadic sunshine can be an inspiration to any budding artist. The sporadic sunshine threw shafts of light through trees and on water surfaces, making brilliant effects of darting streaks of gold and silver and dappled grey-green shadows dancing and leaping all over the place, enhancing the pretty countryside with images of rapidly changing pictures.

On reaching Lower Dale Farm, I left the track and, just past the farm's main entrance, joined the narrow footpath to the right, by a high stone wall and public footpath sign. This path is as narrow as a rabbit track at its start. It follows the river. On the left, across the fields I spotted a large clump of trees known locally as Turncliff Wood. Following the path by the river bank, I noticed a considerable stretch of high ground ahead. Going in this direction you're near to the site of Marple Hall. A headstone and collection of stones indicate the spot where the old hall was situated, in an elevated position over the river valley. It's interesting to note that John Bradshawe, President of the High Court of Justice during the English Civil War who was appointed to try King Charles 1 and, who was the first to sign this tragic king's death warrant, lived at Marple Hall. After the hall had been unoccupied for some considerable time, unfortunately it became a target for vandals so consequently was demolished in the late 1950's.

Before long, I reached the weir with its ancient ford. This weir is wider than the one at the Torrs Riverside Park at New Mills and the water does not tumble down as rapidly nor does it look as spectacular as the Torrs weir. This Marple weir is more tranquil with the river here usually calm as a mill pond but nevertheless attractive in its own way. The weir and ancient bridge are well maintained by the Borough of Stockport as the sign by the bridge indicates. Before the construction of Otterspool Bridge near Wyevale Garden Centre, this was the route that horses and carts used on their way to Romiley.

The path then leads to a stile. Once over the stile there are several rather steep paths up the wooded hillside, most of them leading up to a fence stretching along the top at Dooley Lane. I selected one of the less steep slopes, used the fence as a landmark and kept going to the right when eventually I reached the end of the woodland stretch. I hopped over a low stile along the public footpath leading across the field and onto Dooley Lane and the next place close by on the right is Wyevale car park and its Garden Centre.

I was really glad to reach this excellent place where I cleaned the mud off my boots in their well equipped loo, had a quick wash and brush-up and headed for their cafeteria for a well-earned pot of tea and a muffin. For negotiating the quagmire without tripping over and ending up looking like a drenched, mud-caked alien I even treated myself to a "Sounds of the Sea to Music" CD from their "Sounds of Nature" CD Sale!

Discovery Trails

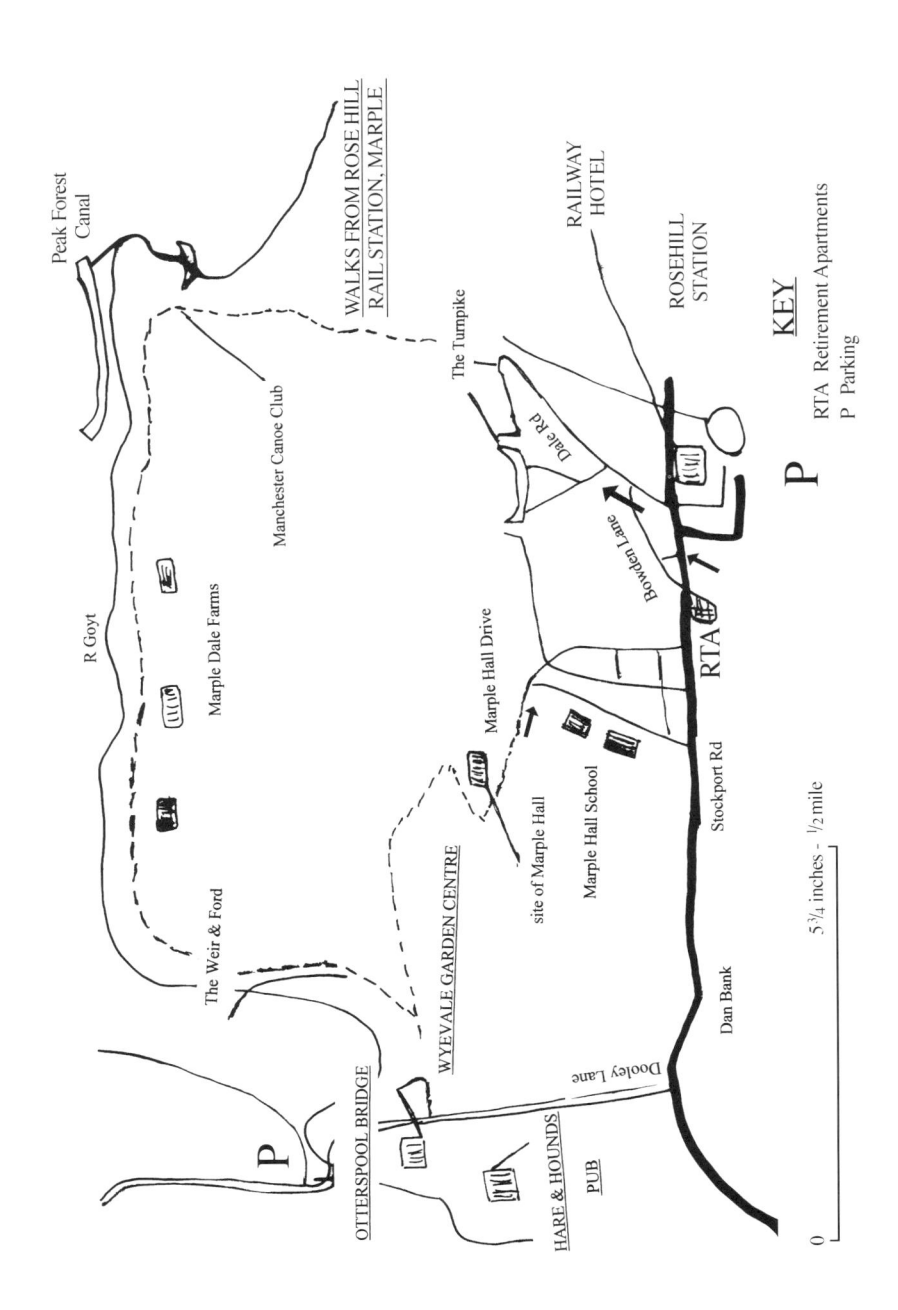

High Life! Over the Tops at Glossop – Thursday 2nd March 2004

Facilities: Pubs and cafes in Glossop and nearby Hadfield which are most suitable for use by disabled people are as follows: The George on Norfolk St, Glossop Cafeteria on Victoria St, The Nag's Head on Charlestown Rd, Café' Nouveau in Co-op Superstore, Tesco Supermarket café' on High St West, The Chieftain and The Pear Tree – both these last named are in Hadfield. Many other pubs and cafes in and around the town.

Public toilets: Behind the indoor market and facing the yard at the town hall. Disabled Accessible toilets in Market Place and Manor Park, Glossop.

Public transport links: Bowers **61** bus Glossop-Buxton, **61A** Peak Bus Network Glossop-Huddersfield (Sundays and Bank Holiday service), **394** Speedwell Glossop-Hazel Grove (terminates and picks up at Stepping Hill Hospital –no Sunday or Bank Holiday Monday service but there is a Saturday service for Good Friday), **236** & **237** Stagecoach Glossop-Manchester via Ashton-under-Lyne.

Rail service: From Manchester Piccadilly to Glossop/Hadfield via Broadbottom.

This particular walk would not be suitable for anyone who has mobility problems. However, Glossop Tourist Information Centre at The Gatehouse Victoria St (Tel No 01457 855920) can advise visitors as to which of the many walks around Glossop and Hadfield are on relatively flat terrain and which would be wheelchair friendly.

On a sharp, chilly but clear morning with the sun's rays trying hard to break through the clouds, I met a small, cheerful group of rangers and ramblers at Glossop Rail Station which is next door to the Co-op buildings. The two rangers were from New Mills and Glossop respectively. Also present was Alice Wright, who was, at that time, our local Health Walks Co-ordinator.

Glossop Railway Station is quite historic, dating from 1847, when the 13th duke of Norfolk led the way in developing a branch line from Manchester to Glossop to save the town from missing out on a vital trade link for the town's mills therefore avoiding economic depression and unemployment. Notice the duke's own private entrance to the station; it has the Howard lion crest over its doorway.

From the rail station we turned left into Howard St, then right into Talbot St, then left at the end of Talbot St and onto Fauvel Rd, passing the Adult Education Centre and Public Library, then left again onto Talbot Rd. From the middle of Talbot Rd, a narrow uphill path took us onto a picturesque, prosperous-looking, private estate, then through another narrow access gimmel with steps and a somewhat wonky handrail which, in turn, led us up onto Heath Rd. When you climb up here the views become ever more spectacular as you ascend; indeed the dramatic Pennines are never far away.

From the middle part of Heath Rd, turning right, we climbed up Fernhill Close and, at the top of Fernhill Close, turned right for Bowden Rd. At the end of Bowden Rd we went ahead for a few yards then turned left into Bexley Close. On the right is an area known as The Heath where there are large impressive-looking stone buildings on both sides of the path. The buildings are the Heath Farm Stables. Although in a ye olde world style they looked fairly new and, judging by their appearance, looked prosperous.

Keeping straight ahead, we continued uphill along a straggling footpath. This hill, which bends gradually to the right, is Winberry Hill. On its right-hand side is a small but well stocked garden centre. As we climbed higher, an interesting-looking prefab-like building came into view on the horizon. Dave, our cheerful group leader, explained that it was firstly an atomic then a nuclear shelter bunker for protection against either of these attacks and was used by the local Civil Defence League back in the Cold War days. (Aldermaston, Ban the Bomb demonstrations and all that. Brought back memories for some members of our party!) The path, on its last section before it joins on to Cemetery Rd at the top, had overgrown hedges on both sides so we proceeded carefully here to avoid being hit and scratched by overhanging, prickly branches and twigs.

Once on Cemetery Rd, the view is a truly magnificent one with a moorland panorama stretching from Shire Hill over to Broom Hill and Cat Wood to the east. From Cemetery Rd, also to the east, there's a good view of the B6105 Woodhead Rd via Torside Reservoir which joins up with the A6024 road at Woodhead Pass. These roads straddle the famous Longdendale Valley with its fir trees and reservoirs with their grey-green, glassy surfaces, looking from this distance like mini mirrors sporadically dotted on the moors almost as if a giant hand had thrown them from a great height. To the west is the district of Padfield, quite an extensive, built-up area the size of a large village when seen from this viewpoint.

At the junction of Cemetery Rd and Park Rd, we turned left onto Hilltop Rd, then followed a narrow track ahead which bent slightly to the right, taking us onto Castlehill Wood where the TV mast for Glossop is situated. It's a lovely spot with mixed deciduous and fir tree woodland, a profusion of wild flowers and a panoramic view over Glossop and the Higher Dinting area near to where the vintage steam trains and engines used to be on display for the railway enthusiasts. Unfortunately the Dinting Vale Railway Museum closed down in the late 1980's having had a struggle to keep attracting visitors, especially the wider public, due to its specialist nature. The premier locomotive Bahamas and its preservation society of the same name are now at the Keighley and Worth Valley Steam Railway.

Castlehill Wood is an ideal place for local people and visitors alike to relax and get way from the hurly-burly of urban life. On this day of our walk, the intermittent rain had cleared and the weather had brightened up considerably so we enjoyed the added bonus of this spot being bathed in sunshine.

After a short but pleasant break we walked downhill along the aptly named Hilltop Rd which has attractive scenery despite being built-up and somewhat suburban in places. If you go walking/cycling up here the wonderful panoramic moorland views are still visible along most of this road.

From here we went through Ashes Lane, then left into Dinting Lane and back into Glossop via High Street West, thence to Henry St and Glossop Rail Station. **The verdict:** a most enjoyable, worthwhile ramble with good company all the way. I strongly recommend anyone new to walking and with leisure time to spare at either weekdays or occasional weekends, to join one of your local organised health walks as they are a great way to keep fit inexpensively. They're also ideal to stimulate interest in countryside conservation and make new friends. You don't even have to book on them - just turn up on the day. Information leaflets containing lists of these walks, dates, times, routes, etc are available from your local town hall, tourist information centres, heritage centres, community/leisure centres- in fact any appropriate information outlet.

Discovery Trails

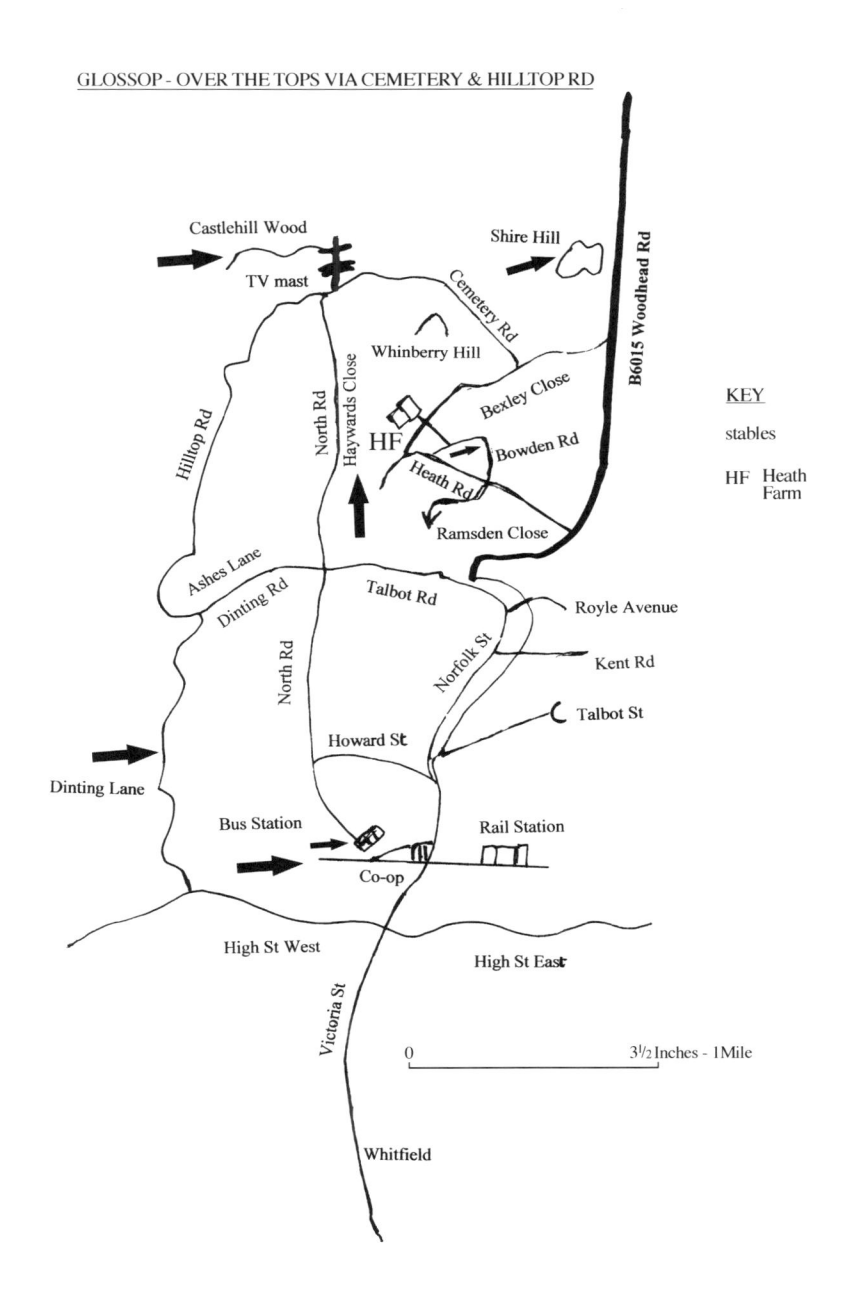

GLOSSOP - OVER THE TOPS VIA CEMETERY & HILLTOP RD

Round A Staffordshire Moorland Gem – Tittesworth Reservoir

Distance: 5 miles each way from Meerbrook Village Hall and all round the reservoir to the Visitor Centre. From the Visitor Centre, there are 2 trails round different parts of the reservoir. Both these walks are shorter than starting out from Meerbrook. From the village hall to the reservoir's dam is also a very pleasant walk, being 1 ¾ miles each way.

Facilities: Refreshments – The Lazy Trout pub at Meerbrook and Tittesworth Visitor Centre café. Large car park at the centre plus children's playground and sandpit.

Toilets: (included those suitable for disabled visitors) in the Visitor Centre. Also extra toilets (inc another disabled one) around the bird hides, a short distance behind the Visitor Centre. Easy wheelchair access into centre.

Public transport links: Buses - First **PMT X18** runs between Hanley and Sheffield, calling at Buxton and Leek 4 times per day each way. (also Sunday and B. H. Monday service). **221** Taxico service from Leek – runs on Summer Saturdays, Sundays and B. H. Mondays.

Motorists: Use A53 Buxton-Leek road. If approaching Tittesworth from Buxton – turn right at Upper Hulme. There's also some off road parking at The Roaches (fantastic rock formations) about 1 mile from Tittesworth.

For this walk on 7th April 2004, I joined the Peak Park Rangers as this Tittesworth ramble was offered as one on their list of leisure walks for the year. The Peak Park Rangers are based in Bakewell but arrange pick-up points by minibus at Buxton, Doveholes and Chapel-en-le-Frith. They are a most friendly, helpful and dedicated group as are the New Mills/Hayfield Health Walks team in High Peak. I have equal admiration and praise for them both.

After being picked up in Buxton, my fellow walkers and I arrived at Meerbrook Village Hall for refreshments and to meet with our group leaders for what proved to be an interesting and lovely scenic trail round Tittesworth Reservoir, one of Staffordshire Moorlands area's popular tourist attractions near The Roaches rocks and the village of Meerbrook, which also has its own reservoir and the rivers nearby – the Churnet and a network of streams, tributaries of the river Dane, where anglers enjoy trout fishing – hence the comical and aptly named village pub, the Lazy Trout.

We turned right just outside the village hall and went down the village road, crossed over to the main Leek road and followed it straight ahead until we turned slightly left onto a country track leading to North Hillswood Farm. A short way down the track we passed an ancient barn and were then treated to a glorious, clear view over Tittesworth Reservoir. Our leader pointed out two rock formations to the left of the reservoir, a good way in the distance but still near enough to enjoy a clear view of them. One was Hen Cloud, a weird shape indeed; it looked just like the head of a cock rooster perched at a lopsided angle. Hen Cloud is part of a weathered gritstone ridge known as The Roaches, a prominent landmark facing north-west and close to the A53 Buxton-Leek road. These rocks have worn into fantastic and comical shapes; one like a lion's head, a human face with a winking eye when the sun and shadows are in the right place, a spinning top, a serpent and so on – they're a photographer and artist's quirky dream. Their name is derived from Norman French 'rocher' meaning rock and were so called by the Gallic monks who constructed and founded De La Cresse Abbey, a mile north of Leek. The Roaches, Ramshaw Rocks (line of jagged, vertical gritstone rocks like fortifications), Meerbrook and Tittesworth – in fact this whole area was once part of the Swythamley Estate around Macclesfield Forest, the territory of the Brocklehurst family.

In 1980 this area was purchased by the Peak District National Park for £180,000. Next, its crumbling footpaths were rebuilt and then it was opened up to the public. The land around Tittesworth Reservoir is now owned and controlled by Severn Trent Water Company and the farms dotted round the estate are in individual private ownership.

Returning to our ramble: the track wound on, past the farm and gradually down to the woodlands and, slightly to the right, emerged a view of the pleasant market town of Leek. Snaking round a little to the left, the woodland path its tiny, clear, fast-running brooks darting alongside, looping their way between clumps of trees, led down to the shores of Tittesworth. It should be noted that the paths leading to and the ones around the reservoir can be muddy and slippery after spells of wet weather so should these conditions prevail, sturdy tough boots or shoes are recommended. Keeping straight ahead along the reservoir shore there are a few steps to descend, sloping down to the pumping station and the large, prominent dam stretching across to the east bank.

Here, perched on the ledge of the stone wall, we enjoyed our packed lunches and our usual, friendly natter exchanged between rangers and us occasional walkers. Our leader mentioned that, when using the trails along Tittesworth's shores, it's interesting to note that the east and west banks of this reservoir differ from one another regarding their trees. The west bank has a greater variety as Hinds Clough Wood (don't think it has quite 57 varieties though!), an ancient woodland is situated on this bank. It supports many deciduous trees including ash, oak, birch, elm, rowan, sycamore, holly, hazel, elder and hybrid limes. However, the east bank has more conifer plantations containing pine and larch trees.

After lunch I and a few other members of our party pleaded guilty to "chickening out" and accepted a lift in the land rover to the visitor centre, offered by our chief ranger as it had begun to rain and remained cold for the time of year. The other, more intrepid walkers proceeded up the steps by the landscaped area with its recently planted trees, to the other side of the reservoir.

On our way to the visitor centre, along the main road, our ranger pointed out two log cabin style buildings from which this area's ranger network organise the duke of Edinburgh's Award Scheme for young people who choose outdoor pursuits/countryside and nature conservation as subjects in which to gain certificates. Youngsters who have special needs can also study for the award subject to supervision if appropriate. While at school, my elder daughter Sarah (who has Asperger's Syndrome) achieved one for volunteering skills/service in her local community. A highly commendable scheme from which all communities benefit including the young people themselves.

Once at the visitor centre we all enjoyed browsing round the exhibitions and gift shop as well as a welcome cuppa and homemade cake at the centre's excellent self service restaurant. Tittesworth visitor centre, its reservoir and surrounding area makes a wonderful day out for everyone who loves the countryside provided, of course, that the weather behaves reasonably well. In addition to facilities and attractions already listed under the introductory information, there is a delightful sensory garden, conservation area and bird hides, all within the visitor centre's grounds. Whilst we were at the centre, extensive work was being carried out on the footpaths in its grounds with the objective of improving disabled access even more than its present good provision. Tittesworth Centre is especially good for family days out as there's no admission charge to view the exhibitions. In particular, the interactive water exhibition provides thought-provoking fun for children and teenagers alike. From this centre the local rangers also run a full programme of activities throughout the year. Details and bookings are available at reception.

As this reservoir is noted for its plentiful stocks of rainbow trout, brown trout, perch and roach, fishing from its banks and boats is available from early morning until one hour after sunset, from March to October. For further details ring 01538 300389.

Tittesworth provides a wide variety of habitats for an equally diverse population of animals, plants and wild flowers along its shores, there being several woodland areas, grassland, meadows, brooks and streams.

Wildlife seen around the shores and woodlands at Tittesworth
<u>Spring</u> Dunlin, greenshank, common sandpiper, heron, whimbrel.
<u>Summer</u> Willow warbler, coal tit, goldcrest.
<u>Winter</u> Wildfowl – Canada goose, pochard, tufted duck, widgeon.
<u>Wild Animals</u> Badger (nocturnal), fox, mouse, shrew, red deer, vole, wild rabbit.

Altogether it's nature's hypermarket!

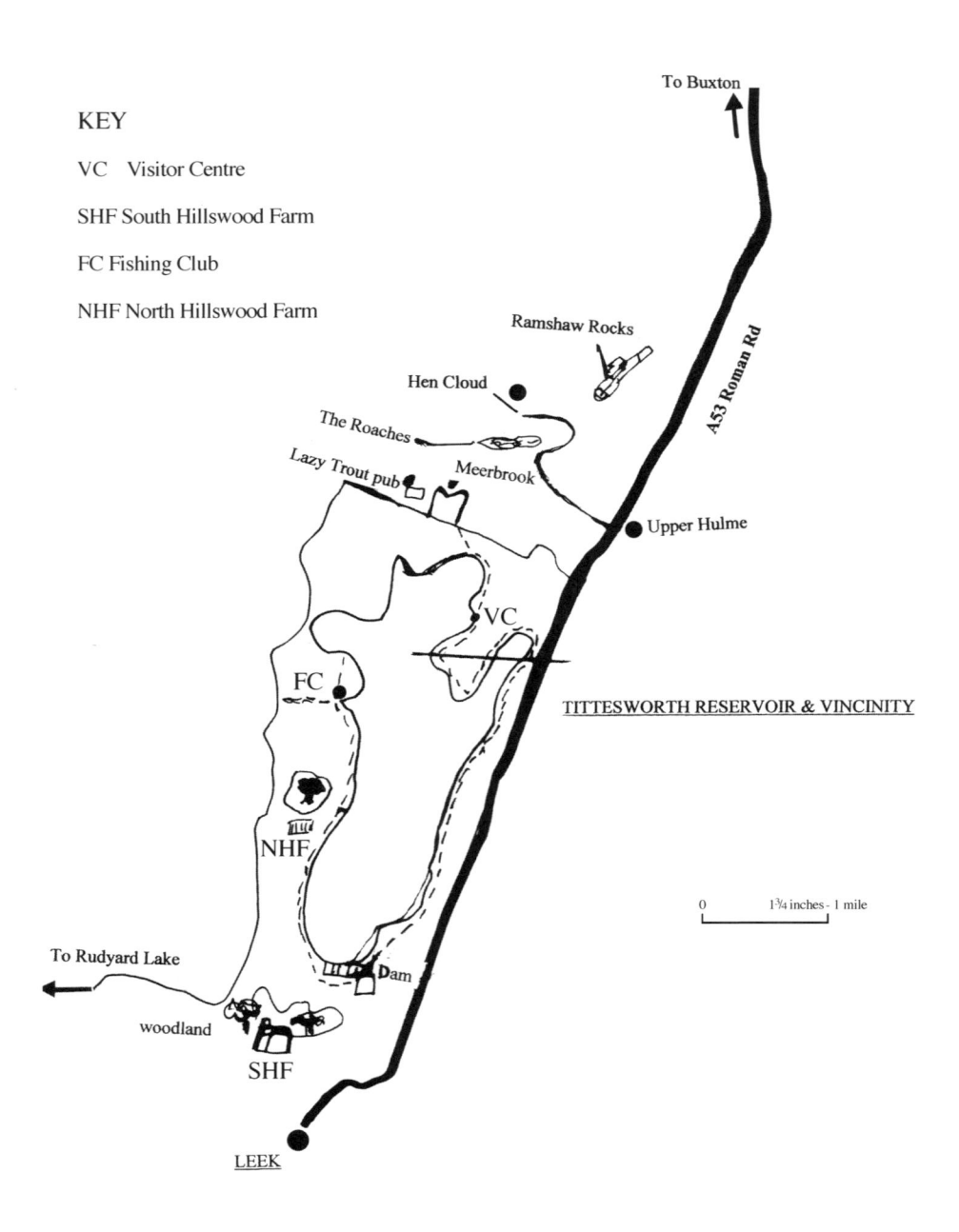

Discovery Trails

KEY

VC Visitor Centre

SHF South Hillswood Farm

FC Fishing Club

NHF North Hillswood Farm

TITTESWORTH RESERVOIR & VINCINITY

Little Hayfield Moorland Taster

Distance: About 1 mile each way.

Facilities: Public toilets at Information Point in Hayfield. Situated at Hayfield former railway station at the end of the Sett Valley Trail. Large car park. Also refreshment kiosk, shop and picnic tables.

Pubs with disabled access: In Hayfield: The Bull's Head, The George Hotel, Kinder Lodge, The Sportsman, The Royal Hotel - last named establishment (Accessible toilet – women's only) Lantern Pike at Glossop Rd, Little Hayfield.

Public transport links: Buses - **361** Stagecoach Stockport-Glossop (no Sunday or Bank Holiday service) **61** Bowers Buxton-Glossop, **61A** Peak Bus Network Huddersfield-Buxton via Holmfirth & Glossop (Sunday & Bank holiday service).

N.B. This short moorland walk from Park Hall Estate buildings would not be suitable for people with mobility problems due to the hill walking involved. However, from the centre of Hayfield the Kinder Trail has a good level path up to the campsite. Through the exit gate and onto Edale Rd there's some seating and waterfalls to admire (see Hayfield Moorland Taster article in contents list)

On Spring Bank Holiday Monday, 31st May 2004, my daughter Sarah and I caught the local 61 Buxton-Glossop Bowers bus to Little Hayfield, alighting at the stop opposite the main gates of Park Hall National trust country estate. A short way through took us to a most impressive stone mansion with large Grecian columns at each side of a huge picture window. A little further along, the path wound its way through a clump of woodland to another smaller but equally impressive stone palladium style building again with even more large Grecian columns on this one. They were all along the front, save the middle section where the door was situated. The second Greek temple cum mansion house looked, on balance, to be the estate office. All around us were clumps of deep pink, red and lilac rhododendrons in full bloom, adding a colourful dimension to an already lovely country scene. With it being such a bright, sunny day, the artist in me wanted to draw, paint and frame the scene within the not-too-distant future. We saw two peacocks but on this occasion they avoided spreading out their famous fantails.

Park Hall in the 18th and early 19th century was lived in by two distinguished local characters, Joseph Hague, entrepreneur and philanthropist, whose educational trust is still active today and in the first half of the following century, Captain John White, public-spirited landowner and dare-devil jockey. In the early part of the 20th century, Park Hall was also used to provide free holidays for poor and handicapped people from Manchester. As part of its renovation in the 1930's, a large, luxury swimming pool was built in the grounds where the public could swim and sunbathe in beautiful surroundings with panoramic moorland views to admire. Large trees screened the pool's area thus ensuring privacy for all concerned. A grand place indeed, offering the best of all worlds for its lucky guests.

At the end of the path, the National Trust signs pointed both left and right. Also, directly in front of us was a signpost marked "Middle Moor". The left hand signpost leads on to William Clough and Kinder Reservoir via White Brow. The route then follows the path along Marepiece Wood back to Bowden Bridge and the old quarry car park of the same name where the plaque commemorating the famous Kinder Mass Trespass of 1932 is displayed. From there the path leads back onto Kinder Rd. This particular walk is a longer, more ambitious one (4 $1/2$ miles) than the one we did on this day.

We turned right and followed the stony moorland path leading upwards towards the Snake Path. As we climbed to the top of this path, we enjoyed a good view of the hill called Lantern Pike on the opposite side of the valley. The hill and its beacon is a helpful landmark for walkers. In the area is a local inn of the same name which is popular with visitors all the year round. At the top we were treated to a wonderful view of the wide, far flung, colourful moorland carpeted with wiry green/gold grass, yellow gorse and purple heather scattered in irregular clumps over the whole scene.

Through the gate, at the top of this section of the path, we crossed a wide field, then alongside a tall, drystone wall to a gate and stile at the top, leading to another field sloping downhill. As we descended we joined the prominent, narrow path aptly named the Snake Path as it literally winds down to the large clump of trees. This is the popular Hayfield landmark named Twenty Trees from which you can see a splendid view of Hayfield with its quaint old stone buildings and the turret-like tower of its parish church.

Snake Path, opened in the 1890's, was the first official footpath over to Kinderscout, thanks to persistent campaigning by the Northern Counties Footpath Society. At the start of this path on Kinder Rd, look out for the metal sign indicating thus. This was the beginning of our nation's ramblers challenge to authority for freedom to walk on the moors.

Another downhill, winding, short walk below Twenty Trees brought us back onto Kinder Rd, then into Bank St and thence into the village centre where, on what turned out to be a hot, sunny day, a very welcome choice of pubs were all invitingly open for that essential long, cool lager, lemonade or whatever takes your fancy as long as it's a generous amount, cool and thirst-quenching!

Discovery Trails

PARK HALL, MIDDLE MOOR & HAYFIELD

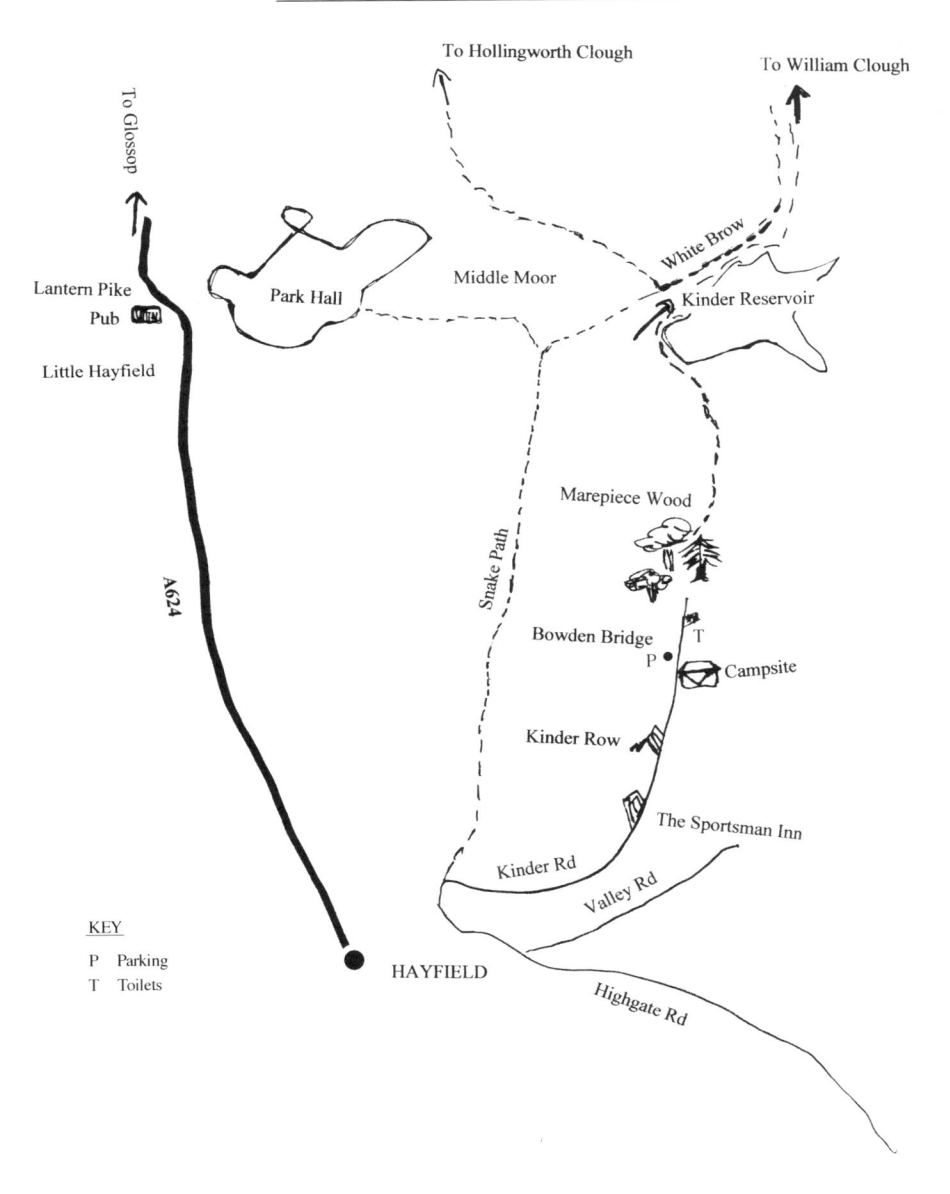

To Hollingworth Clough
To William Clough
To Glossop
Lantern Pike Pub
Little Hayfield
Park Hall
Middle Moor
White Brow
Kinder Reservoir
A624
Marepiece Wood
Snake Path
Bowden Bridge
Campsite
Kinder Row
The Sportsman Inn
Kinder Rd
Valley Rd
HAYFIELD
Highgate Rd

KEY
P Parking
T Toilets

77

Meandering Along Goyt Way to Mouseley Bottom & The Goytside Meadows Nature Reserve.

Distance: About 1 mile each way from New Mills town centre.

Access routes to the Reserve: The two routes which disabled people could use are as follows: From New Mills Newtown Rail Station, turn right onto Albion Rd, then up the side street marked Victoria St which leads onto the canal towpath via Victoria Wharf. A short distance down this public footpath takes you onto the Reserve via the Meadow Path or you can keep to the left along the Pasture Path and then turn right along the link path to join the Meadow Path and Broad Walk. This way is relatively direct but care needs to be taken going down the public footpath leading from the canal as it's uneven in places.

There's also access to the reserve from the car park at Hague Bar Picnic Site by keeping to the path which is close to the river banks via two "kissing gates" which follow on from one another and leading to Mouseley Bottom. Note that this route should be avoided after spells of wet weather as the path will then be very muddy and slippery.

Other options: From New Mills town centre bus station or car parks, walk down into the Torrs Gorge cross the Millenium Bridge and then go across the Millward footbridge walking by the river up to Goytside Farm, turning right onto the Reserve.

You can also join the path at the end of Griffin Close by walking down to the end of New St in the Church Rd area of the town. As an alternative starting point, parking is available en route at the Co-op Pioneers Supermarket car park on Church Rd. Keeping to the left, walk down under the railway bridge to Goytside Farm and over that same footbridge which takes you onto the Goyt Way (alternatively named Midshires Way) leading to the Reserve. These 2 last named alternative routes are not suitable for disabled people as the paths to and from the footbridge are narrow and often muddy after rain. Our local access group are trying to negotiate with the council for the paths to be re-surfaced. The bridge itself is currently under reconstruction, good progress is being made and the work should be completed soon including access for wheelchairs. However the section of the path which winds round the rear of Goytside Farm and crosses this bridge is closed until 1 November 2005 for safety reasons while construction work is being carried out.

Please note: At present there is no parking available near the

Reserve. However, our local access group have recently contacted New Mills Town Council for 2 parking bays for use by disabled people to be provided at this end of the Torrs Riverside Park. They are hoping for a positive reply in the near future.

Public transport links: Buses: 361 Stagecoach Stockport-Glossop, **358** Stagecoach Stockport-Hayfield via Marple, **355** Bowers Marple-Hayfield (no weekend service), **61** & **61A** Buxton-Huddersfield (as with the other buses these 2 last-named stop at New Mills Bus Station).
By Rail: From New Mills Newtown Station Northern Trains Buxton-Stockport, Sheffield-Manchester Northern Trains stops at New Mills Central Station.

As the weather during the first week of October, 2004 had remained bright, clear and dry, the odds seemed in my favour to take a Sunday afternoon walk to our new local nature reserve at Goytside Meadows. The reserve is situated at the southern end of the Torrs Riverside Park (Grid Ref: SK001847). There are several ways into this pretty, tranquil area as listed above.

I chose to go down the path leading from New Mills Central Station to the valley bottom. It's quite steep but there is a handrail on its left-hand side. On route is the lovely river and woodland scenery of the Torrs Gorge area – note the Millward wooden footbridge across the river, to the left, with its foamy weir, silver ripples and darting shadows of sunlight and shade, creating silver foil, pale gold and dark green alternating colour effects. At the valley bottom is a small parking area and two signposts marked "Goyt Way," pointing in opposite directions. I took the left-hand turning and, as I made my way towards the woods around Mouseley Bottom, I glimpsed, through the trees lining the route, the attractive clearing, landscaped like a new country park with the new millennium trees thriving very well. The path wound round the construction site still here as this end of the Torrs is in the process of ongoing development following from the opening of the award-winning Millennium Walkway. I opened the steel-levered site's gate from which the path snaked in a circle then split into two turnings left and right. Again I took the left turning, joining the path through the woods which brought me to a tall gate and stile to the left which, in turn, led to Mouseley Bottom.

The woodland walks are part of this conservation area which has recently seen some interesting developments. Walking through the woods I spotted ash, birch, silver birch, sycamore and a couple of oak trees. On the ground, in random clumps like a domino effect, were small clusters of wild flowers with rounded petals of white with a pinkish hue like cross-stained white garments in the wash. This is Himalayan Balsam, a high ground loving plant, often seen in hilly or mountainous parts of our world. Before this woodland was managed the trees grew too close together, shutting out light and overcrowding the ground below. Notices are dotted around the woodland, displaying details of what is being done to remedy this problem by way of ongoing conservation work which involves clearing some areas by felling a number of trees to make space for light and growth of shrubs, wild flowers for insects to pollinate, more habitats for birds, hedgehogs, badgers, squirrels, etc. The New Mills/Hayfield Rangers also plan to introduce hazel, rowan and some trees of the spruce family to ensure a good mix of woodland within the Mouseley Bottom conservation area. The conservation project organised by Derbyshire Countryside Services and financed by the Forestry Commission is now completing its first year in operation and has another three years to run. When one stops to think about environmental improvements, the reclamation of this whole area is a remarkable achievement as it once was the town's refuse tip. It's a most encouraging testimony of what can be done when local authorities, countryside governing bodies and community groups liase and work together to enrich our environment.

To return to my mini ramble; at the end of the path I crossed over a short clearing where there was yet another Goyt Way signpost to a stile opposite the woods which you climb over to enter Mouseley Bottom. It's a sturdy stile with two secure footholds so it's relatively easy to use. Once over the stile I came to an attractive circular stretch of parkland which is a bird sanctuary. On the right-hand side is the Derbyshire Countryside Services Ranger Hut with bird hides at its rear end. There's also a small notice up on the information board near the hut about this spot being popular with bramblings. Apart from a small picture of one, there isn't much other information about them. I subsequently discovered through enquiring with a local bird-watching expert to whom I'm much obliged for these interesting facts, that these bramblings have also been at another New Mills park namely High Lea Park just off St Mary's Rd, which is opposite the bus station. Bramblings are a delightful addition to Mouseley Bottom. They have chestnut and white markings particularly noticeable on their rumps when they take off in flight. They are social birds who often keep company with chaffinches. Only occasionally is one seen alone. They feed on the ground under beech trees. Bramblings migrate from the northern end of Scandinavia to Britain for the winter months. Britain in winter time hardly springs to mind as a warm, sunny holiday destination but, to these birds from near the Arctic Circle, our country must have for them, the Riviera touch!

From Mouseley Bottom, two routes, the pasture path and the meadow path, both signposted clearly, link the meadows with the public footpath along the Peak Forest Canal to the right of Albion Rd, entrance via Victoria St. The meadows look colourful in all seasons barring winter as many varieties of wild flowers grow there. In October the aptly named Autumn Hawkbit, just starting to bloom in the reserve's extensive grassland on this Sunday walk, formed a carpet of orange and gold, tiny daisy-like flowers to delight the eye. This wild flower is named after its sharp pointed leaves, resembling a hawk's beak.

New Mills nearly lost these wonderful meadows as, in the early 1990's, they were acquired by the Highways Agency because of being on the favoured route for a planned five lane by-pass of the A6. Strong opposition from the local community forced the agency to abandon this plan and so, consequently, New Mills Town Council purchased the land from the Highways Agency and, when they bought a further area of land from a local farmer, started work on creating this local nature reserve. It was designated a Local Nature Reserve in 2003. It's now jointly owned and managed by New Mills Town Council Town Council and Derbyshire County Council. The Town Council works in liason with local farmers whose animals graze on the Reserve, munching the grass to stimulate regular new vegetation growth which, in turn, encourages good quality habitat for insects and a good, ecological balance all round. It's worth remembering that parts of the Reserve are often wet even in dry weather so you need to keep to the paths. The best time to visit Goytside Meadows is between April and October because of the colourful displays of wild flowers there and obvious factors like more daylight and less slippery underfoot.

On the right-hand side of Mouseley Bottom, coming down from the Central Station path or the Millennium Bridge, there is a path leading on to Hague Bar Picnic Site which makes a pleasant country walk, wooded in parts. There's also a right-hand path which soon leads to the River Goyt's banks. The river footpath also brings you out close to Hague Bar Picnic Site and is a super walk for spotting birds and wild flowers along the river banks. Moorhens, mallard ducks, sand martins and kingfishers are all known to nest here.

I returned via Mouseley Bottom and the Millennium Bridge then a short way from this bridge, on the left, I went up the steps signposted to the Heritage Centre and back into the town after an enjoyable walk.

Discovery Trails

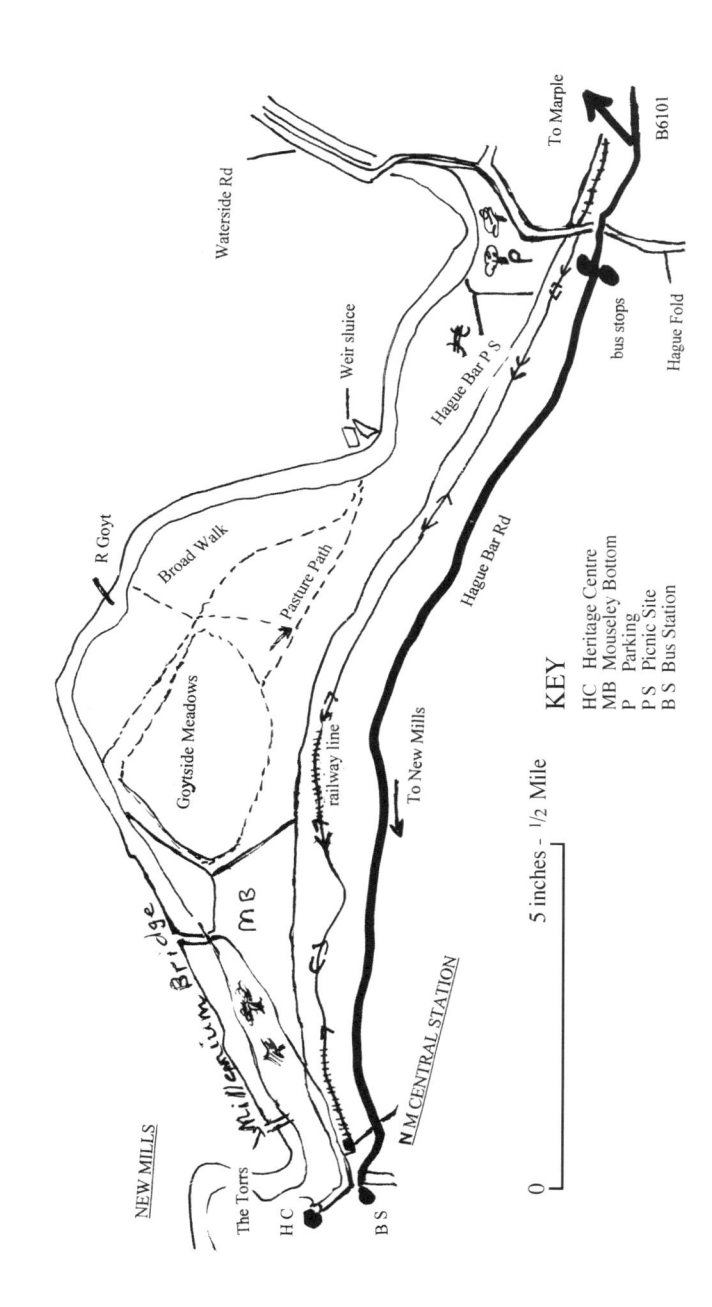

85

Around Hope

Distances: From railway station to Hope Village is _ a mile each way. From public footpath on Eccles Lane to Navio Roman Fort at Brough – 1 mile each way.
From Pindale Rd along banks of Peakshole Water to Castleton – 1 mile.

Facilities: Public toilets at Castleton Rd, Hope and Buxton Rd, Castleton car parks. Both toilets are accessible for disabled people. Level surfaces at both car parks. (smooth tarmac) Hope car park free to disabled badge holders. At each car park, 2 spaces are reserved for disabled people close to the toilets. RADAR KEY required at both toilets.

Refreshments: Various cafes and pubs in and around Hope and Castleton. Most disabled friendly eateries are Savoire-Fare, The Old Hall Inn and The Poachers in Hope and The Castle, Cryer House and The Stables in Castleton.

Public transport links: Buses: Hulleys **173** Castleton-Bakewell, **174** TM Travel Matlock-Castleton, Hulleys **177** Castleton-Bakewell (no Sunday or BH Monday service), TM Travel **202** Castleton-Mansfield (Sundays & BH only), **272** First South Yorkshire Castleton-Sheffield, **273** & **274** Stagecoach East Midlands Castleton-Sheffield, **279** Stagecoach East Midlands Castleton-Chesterfield, **373** Speedwell Manchester-Castleton via Glossop (weekends only).
Rail: Sheffield-Manchester Northern Train Service via New Mills Central Station.

During the half term holiday in late October 2004, I did some exploring in and around the lovely, historic village of Hope, sometimes appearing to be overshadowed by its famous neighbouring village, Castleton, where all the equally famous caves are situated. However, Hope has some fine, attractive buildings, unusual historic features and lovely scenery surrounding it, with a wide choice of country walks, both short, medium and long, easy, moderate or challenging, according to preference and ability.

On this ramble I caught the Sheffield train from New Mills Central Station, alighted at Hope, crossed over the bridge and turned right onto the station path. At the end of this path I turned right again by a row of cottages, walked to the end of this private road and, just past the railway hoardings, joined the slip road up to the main A625, walking towards Hope by the River Noe. (instead of there being Noe Hope the opposite is true, you soon reach Hope by this route!)

On my way into Hope I passed Daggers House with the unusual half moon shaped upper windows and pretty, floral cottage garden. This garden was open to the public during 2003 as the Daggers House residents took part in the Derbyshire Gardens Open for Charity scheme. Hopefully it may be featured again in this most worthwhile venture. Leaflets publicising this annual event can be found in local libraries, tourist information centres, heritage centres, etc throughout the county. Daggers House is 400 years old and still retains some of its original features. The crossed daggers symbol above its door is associated with the cutlers' branch of Sheffield's steel industry and, when Daggers House was an inn, from 1720 to 1860, the transporters of cutlery from Sheffield had probably used this inn on their way to Manchester.

The next interesting building on my discovery trail, a short distance further on is St Peter's Church with its squat Norman tower and ancient churchyard. Unfortunately the building is locked during weekdays so anyone who is interested in discovering more about the church's history would need to visit at weekend when they would find detailed information in its interior. This church owns antique silver artefacts and ancient registers which are displayed in June during Hope Wakes Week. In the churchyard I found the old Saxon Cross, or more accurately, its shaft, close to the south porch by the main pathway. Recent research dates the cross to the 11th century Viking occupation period. This is because of the decoration on its face which is separated, intertwined tracery instead of the continuous tracery in the Saxon style. Mounted on a stone gatepost by Hope Historical Society and near the Saxon cross is an 18th century guidestone, originally found in the vicarage garden. Its hands indicate the route for travelling around Hope and other villages in the Hope Valley on the way to Sheffield.

I then retraced my steps, turned left by the church onto a little, narrow lane that brought me out on Pindale Rd where there's a large signpost pointing uphill to the cement works. Taking the first left turning after the mini-park with the river winding through it and the hump-backed bridge called Watergate, I walked up Eccles Lane, admiring the view over to the church, village and surrounding hills in their cinnamon-gold autumnal glory. A few yards up this lane there's a left-hand turning with a signpost marked 'public footpath to Brough and Navio Roman Fort'. This public footpath is well surfaced and maintained. However, as with all footpaths, care needs to be taken if using them soon after wet weather or snowy/icy conditions. The walk from this point is approximately 1.5 miles each way. On this particular day I decided not to do the Navio walk as time did not permit but I could see from its starting point what a wonderful, scenic ramble it would be. The actual excavated Roman fort was one of a long stretch of forts from the Lincolnshire coast to Merseyside. Navio was part of the Roman Empire's management network for use of local resources which, in this area, was lead. The fort stands on high ground within the curve of the River Noe and Bradwell Brook. Little remains of the actual building except for stones on the ground indicating the site of its headquarters. Nevertheless my little detour round the village footpaths and secondary roads was interesting and fun plus there was much to admire from the artist's point of view.

I continued up Eccles Lane until I reached Eccles House, one of the oldest, officially listed buildings in Hope, ancient documents dating it back to 1306. It was an important post on the ancient route to Bradwell, most likely part of a trading network connected with the lead industry. The building of today was a late 18th century farmhouse until the land was taken over by the cement works. Further recent renovation resulted in Eccles House now containing a business centre. Eccles Lane encircles the village for about a mile but instead of continuing along it I turned back onto Pindale Rd as there's another interesting feature to look at here.

This feature is the Pinfold, a round, drystone walled structure with a rough wooden door, situated on the right-hand side of the road, opposite Watergate Bridge. There's a large, detailed notice inside the Pinfold containing the "Rules for the Pound Keeper". This building was used to keep stray farm/domestic animals until their owner could collect them. The strict Pound Laws extracted a fine from the owner before the official in charge, called the Pinner, would hand their animals over. The rules on the Pinfold notice date from 1947 when, apparently, impounding stray farm animals was steadily becoming obsolete. This was most likely because of increased motorised transport on farms which would obviously make it quicker and easier to find and return missing stock. Even in the days before computers and advanced travel technology, government in general seemed to find it a struggle to keep up with scientific and technical progress within the modern world. This just shows you that there's nothing new under the sun!

Further along, past the Pinfold, still on the right-hand side, where Pindale Rd starts to slope upwards, is a clearly marked public footpath which runs along the banks of the stream known as Peakshole Water, twisting and winding its way into Castleton. Even at the start of this walk, which is just over a mile, the scenery is breathtakingly beautiful. There are extensive panoramic views over to Losehill Hall Study Centre, Losehill Plantation, a narrow strip of woodland on the moors and Losehill itself, towering up above directly to the north.

Nearer to Castleton, another, larger clump of woodland, Brockett Booth Plantation, is visible in the distance just below another well known hill walkers' landmark, Back Tor. When I've walked on these hills around Hope and Castleton in the company of the Peak Park Rangers and friends, there's nothing to beat the marvellous sense of freedom, the spectacular, scenic open spaces to admire, the fresh air and a break from the restrictions of urban life.

Before returning to Hope Station I popped into the Woodroofe Arms, just round the corner from Pindale Rd and adjoining the main A6187 Castleton road. It's an ancient hostelry, dating from the 15th century The inn derives its name from the Woodroofe family; a distinguished local one who played a prominent part in this village's history. They were King's Foresters of the Peak when the Peak Forest was a royal hunting forest occupying most of the Parish of Hope. This original ancient parish was one of the largest in the north of England, stretching from Glossop in the north to Buxton in the south, also from Whaley Bridge in the west to Bamford in the east. They also held the office of Parish Clerk continuously, from father to son, for more than 200 years (1628-1855). Anyway, I can recommend the Woodroofe Arms as it's a friendly, cosy inn which offers tasty, traditional Derbyshire cuisine on its menu.

On the opposite side of the main road, the attractive courtyard is situated. This historic courtyard used to be a stable block and hayloft. Its layout clearly indicates typical features such as feeding booths and stone drinking troughs. There used to be a stylish art gallery here. The building which housed the gallery now has a new function – a bike shop – what a contrast! However, for all lovers of art there is another delightful gallery called The Blue Apple round the next corner on Edale Rd. This one is also as welcoming and friendly as the former Hope Gallery with the same enthusiasm for the beauty and conservation of the Peak District. The rest of Edale Rd is well worth visiting as there are several historic buildings along its way including The Weaver's Cottages situated at the junction of Edale and Castleton Rd where sacking used to be manufactured, the Methodist Chapel dating from 1835 and the Hairdresser's Shop, formerly "The Tin

Hut," believed to be the final survivor of the tin huts brought down from the temporary settlement at Birchinlee in the Upper Derwent Valley, built to house construction workers building Howden and Derwent Dams in the early 20th century.

Discovery Trails

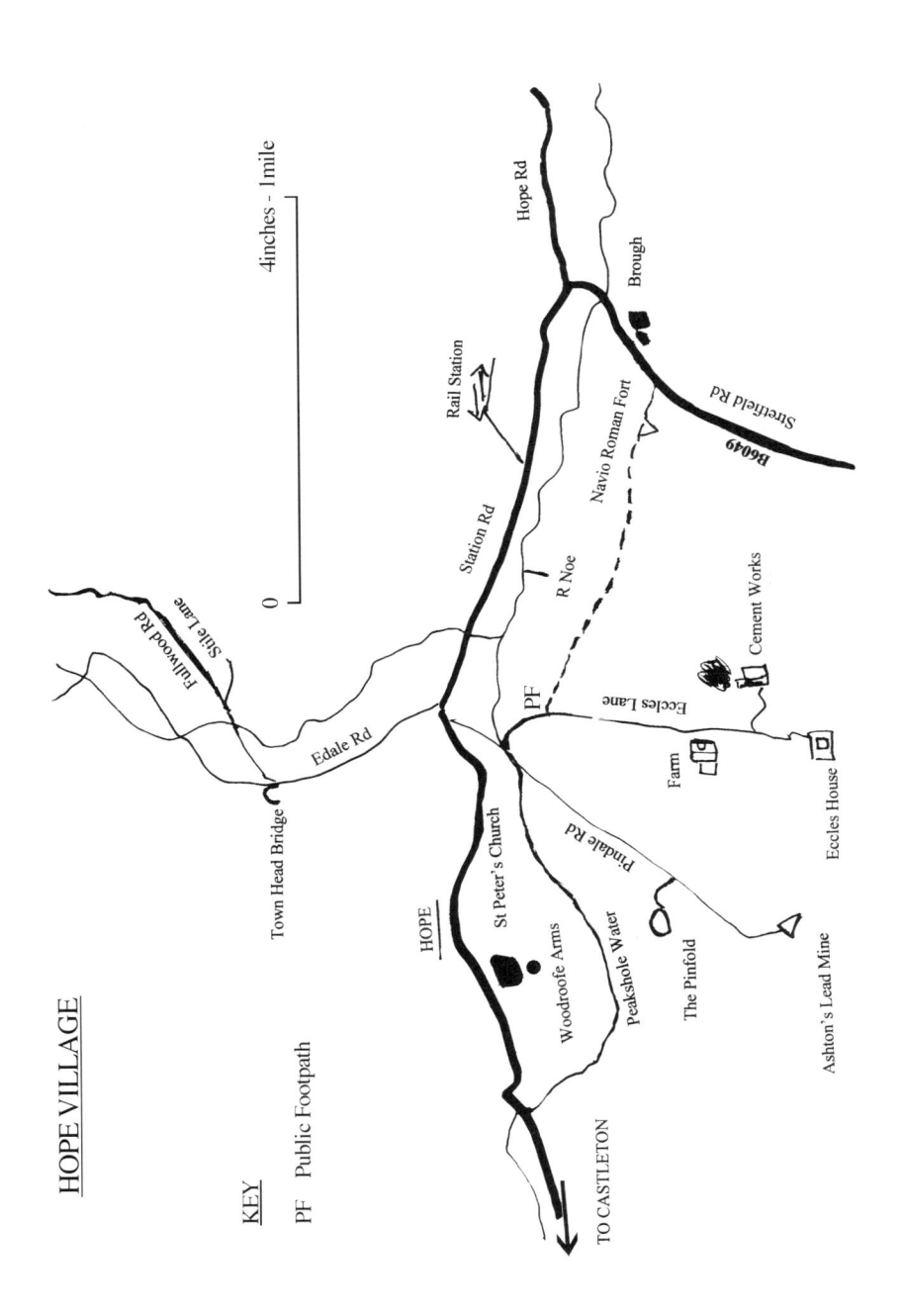

Interesting Facts About Buxton, High Peak's Historic Spa Town

The Romans built a fort, believed to be on the site of Buxton's football ground. They were attracted by the natural thermal springs within the town which remained at the constant temperature of 28°C (82°F). They named the spa Aquae Arnemetiae. Although the Romans are credited with discovering the health-giving waters, the opinion of archaeologists and its ancient place-name both suggest that the site dates from the Iron Age where there would have been a temple dedicated to the Celtic water goddess Arnemetia. The present day well opposite the Crescent where visitors and locals alike often queue up to obtain free spa water, had its ancient Celtic name changed to the Christian one of St Ann's. Its source originates from Poole's Cavern, a natural show cave to the south west of the town where a subterranean spring runs under its chambers.

Buxton's popular stalactite grotto, Poole's Cavern, situated down Green Lane by Grin Low Country Park (park named after local hill) was used during the Iron Age as a shelter and secret refuge for local Celtic tribes probably when disputes occurred between neighbouring tribes. Excavations around the cavern during the 19th and 20th centuries found evidence that the Romans and Celts used the cavern's entrance as a burial chamber. Skulls, loose bones, pottery, bronze jewellery in shapes of sea creatures, weapons and coins have all been uncovered there. Some of these items are on display at Buxton Museum & Art Gallery on Terrace Road, near the town centre.

Buxton's former Devonshire Royal Hospital (named in honour of the same named duke in 1859) now the new High Peak College, part of the University of Derby), is a landmark for visitors to the town because of its huge, iron-framed dome, built back in 1880, which was, at that time, the largest unsupported dome in the world, the architectural wonder of the Victorian era. It spanned 152 ft (46 metres in width). These days it's the second widest unsupported dome in Europe.

Opposite the Crescent is a low stone classical style building (it blends in well with the Grecian neo-classical style Crescent) which used to house the Micrarium where wonders of the natural world were displayed through microscopes. Now this building, renamed The Pump Room as it was originally part of the spa's thermal springs bath system, is used for the annual High Peak area's Art & Crafts Exhibition which is open from April until late autumn. Admission is free and there's a wonderful extensive display of local talent to delight visitors. Many of the high quality items are on sale at reasonable prices.

Opposite the famous Opera House is the hexagonal post box dating from 1867 named a Penfield box after its designer, J W Penfield. The clear cipher on its front reads "V R" – Victoria Regina. It's a splendid period piece, one of around 100 Victorian post boxes still in use in our country.

St Anne's Church on Bath Rd, Higher Buxton is believed to be the oldest building in Buxton though its exact origins are shrouded in mystery. The date inscribed in its porch, 1625, refers to the porch only. It has some fine stained glass windows in its interior.

As you approach Buxton from the Stockport direction along the A6, on the right-hand side of this road, just past the golf course and club house, is a picturesque cottage set well back from the road and visible behind it is an attractive mini estate and St Peter's Church, Fairfield, the name of this extensive suburb of Buxton. The present church dates from the 19th century but there has always been a chapel or church of some kind on this site for 700 years. A few centuries ago this church used to be part of the parish of Hope so special occasion services such as christenings, weddings, funerals and other important parish events were authorised to take place only in the main parish church. This involved long journeys to Hope in all weathers for Fairfield people (naturally after an 11 mile walk or expedition on horseback – horse and cart at best; especially in winter with snow, arctic temperatures, perhaps encounters with wolves en route the people would be getting a bit fed up with this situation!). Therefore a chantry - at first instance, a chapel of ease, served by a local priest (as this was pre-Reformation times) was set up to overcome the problem. (no doubt to the immense relief of Fairfield inhabitants!)

In the later part of the 16th century the parish was struggling to fund the church's upkeep. Fairfield parishioners petitioned Queen Elizabeth 1 for financial aid, resulting in St Peters receiving practical support by a trust being established for the church and almshouses to be administered by The Governors of the Perpetual Chapel of Fairfield which consisted of "six discreet and honest men." This organisation still exists to this day. The present vicar, with whom I had a friendly chat over the phone, had recently appointed his six administrators to fulfil modern day organisation of the church's finances.

By way of contrast, back in the winter of 1973-74, albeit on a temporary basis, Buxton even had its own ghostly visitor – a weird, night flying helicopter. Seven different police forces were involved in the investigation of this strange phenomenon as there were various sightings of it around the Hope Valley area and parts of North Cheshire though Buxton area was undoubtedly its favourite location! However, despite thorough police investigations, its origins and pilot could not be traced so the mystery remains unsolved to this day. It certainly was a unique apparition – indeed a novelty in the annals of supernatural experiences. It would make a good story-line for the X-Files (popular TV sci-fi supernatural series) or a Hollywood sci-fi suspense movie!

There are many more interesting things to discover on a Buxton Town Trail too numerous to mention in this book which will intrigue and delight visitors and locals alike. *Details are available from Buxton Tourist Information Centre in the Crescent -* **Tel No 01298 25106**.

Sources:

A walk Around Buxton by John Merrill 2004 (Internet version).

Look at Buxton – Bessacar Prints, Doncaster, S Yorks.

St Anne's Church booklet by J J Stark.

The story of St Peter's Church, Fairfield – 700th Anniversary Commemoration leaflet. The vicar of this same church (with many thanks for his friendly co-operation).

My own local knowledge.

Ghosts and Legends of the Peak District by David Clarke, 1991.

More Travel Information & Useful Telephone Numbers

Organisation/Service	Telephone Number	Website/Email
Hope Valley & High Peak T P	01663 746 377	
Northern Trains Hotline	0800 528 0200	
Guided Walks Bookings	0845 129 7777	www.hvhptp.org.uk
Folk Trains	0161 242 6296	www.hvhptp.org.uk
Disabled Travel Assistance	0845 60 40 231	
Traveline	0870 608 2 608	www.traveline.org.uk
Derbyshire Public Transport		www.derbyshire.gov.uk/buses
Derbyshire C C Countryside Service	01663 746222	www.derbyshire.gov.uk/countryside
High Peak Walks for Health	0845 129 77 77	
Peak Park L WKS	01629 816288	
Bakewell & Eyam CT	01629 814889	
Castleton Info Centre	01433 620679	www.visitpeakdistrict.com

KEY

CC	County Council
CT	Community Transport
L WKS	Leisure Walks
T P	Transport Partnership

Acknowledgments

Two local artists who did the illustrations, one of whom wishes to remain anonymous and Bronwen Matthews. The former also gave me some useful tips on how to produce good maps. The latter is steadily building up an excellent reputation for her artwork.

A local artist who did the illustrations and assisted with the maps
Access Guide to Eating in Glossop - compiled by Access Group
Access Guide to Eating in Hope Valley - compiled by Access Group
Alice Wright, former co-ordinator for Health Walks High Peak.
Buxton Tourist Information Bureau.
Castleton Tourist Information Centre.
Clive Price, author of "Mostly Downhill in the Dark Peak".
Countryside Access Group – Hope.
Dave Sims, New Mills Ranger for Health Walks High Peak.
Discover Hope – booklet by Hope Historical Society.
Dominic Smith, Policy Officer (Transportation) Stockport MBC.
Dr D Brumhead, Administrator, New Mills Heritage Centre.
Gerald Hancock, Goyt Valley history author.
Glossop Tourist Information Centre.
Goyt Valley visitor guide leaflet produced jointly by Peak District National Park Authority, United Utilities and the Forestry Commission.
Hayfield Civic Trust
Health Walks High Peak (supported by HPBC).
Information Point at former rail station yard, Hayfield.
Joan Potts, bird expert, New Mills Natural History Society.
Keith Holmes, rambler & special needs volunteer from Whaley Bridge.

Macclesfield Canal Society – their short book entitled "The Macclesfield & Upper Peak Forest Canals".
Marple Library.
Mrs J Hallworth Landlady of The Bull's Head, High Lane.
New Mills Access Group (disabled & pushchairs)
New Mills Library.
New Mills Local History Society.
Olive Bowyer, New Mills local historian and author of "Peak Forest Canal, Upper & Lower Levels".
Paul Finn, Chief Ranger, Hayfield.
Peak Park Rangers based in Bakewell.
Richard Doran, Macclesfield & District Ranger.
Roger, Chief Ranger – Staffordshire Moorlands Area.
Rosemary Taylor, keen member of New Mills Local history Society.
Sarah Mellor, my daughter.
Severn Trent Water Co. Rangers at Tittesworth Reservoir
Sir Martin Doughty (English Heritage).

New **BUS** info:-
On Stockport - Glossop routes
361 Stagecoach & 355 Bowers services are withdrawn

Above services are replaced with:-
62 & 62A Bowers & 239 Speedwell.
Frequency similar.

N.B 239 Speedwell bus now runs between Glossop & Ashton-u-Lyne only.

ALPENSTOCK
THE IN PLACE FOR THE OUTDOORS

All brands available

Boot fitting specialist

Mail order

UK's best prices for tents

WALKING CLIMBING SKIING TREKKING
CAMPING MOUNTAINEERING SNOWBOARDING

35 St. Petersgate, Stockport SK1 1DH tel 0161 480 3660 www.alpenstock.co.uk

---

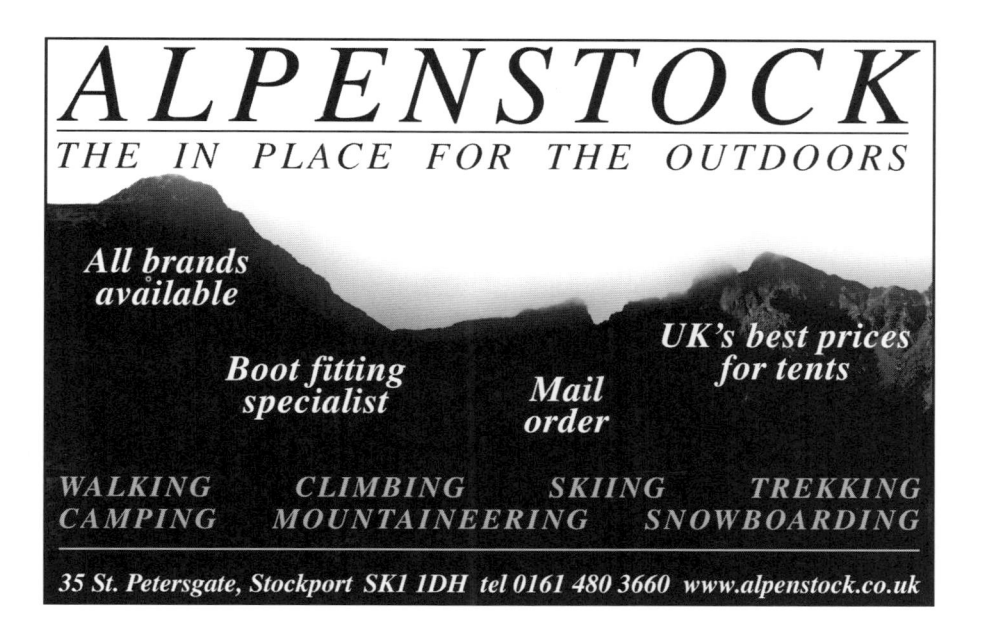

the music studio

Principal: Carolyn Hawkins
G.L.C.M., L.L.C.M.(T.D.), F.L.C.M.

Qualified tuition in Keyboard, Piano, Flute, Clarinet, Guitar, Organ & Theory

49 Albion Road, New Mills, High Peak, Derbyshire, SK22 3EX
Tel: 01663 746226

Whaley Bridge Smithy

A. DEWBERRY

36a 38a Old Road, Whaley Bridge, High Peak, SK23 7HR

☎ 01663 719179

Wrought ironwork, plain & decorative security guards, fence panels, gates, handrails etc.

Picture gates and fence panels,
Sculptures and mobiles a speciality.
Gate automation, rise and fall bollards, and barriers.

Springbank

3 Reservoir Road, Whaley Bridge, High Peak SK23 7BL
Margot Graham 01663 732819 www.whaleyspringbank.co.uk

Quality Victorian style en-suite B & B in the centre of Whaley Bridge

ETC ♦♦♦♦ Guest Accommodation One minute walk from station & bus stop. Local & free range produce used when possible, omnivores & vegetarians equally welcome. Evening meals available by arrangement (or use the dining room for a takeaway). Residents lounge available at all times, TV and hospitality tray in all rooms. Genuine creaky floorboards!

THE BOOK SHOP
(MARPLE) LTD.
70 STOCKPORT ROAD, MARPLE

LATEST PUBLICATIONS
REFERENCE BOOKS
CHILDRENS BOOKS
MAPS

ORDERS WELCOME

TEL: 0161 427 4921

Spinney Cottage

Bed & Breakfast

◊ ◊ ◊ ◊ 4 Diamond Standard Accommodation

Situated 1 mile from the picturesque village of Hayfield. Panoramic views over the surrounding Peak District.

Double room en-suite, twin room en-suite and single room with private bathroom. Cosy dining dining/sitting room for use by guests.

Open all year round except Christmas & New Year

Tariff £25.00 per person, per night

Prop: Mrs. J. Waterhouse.   Tel: 01663 743230

Griff
Guest House

2 Compton Road
BUXTON
Derbyshire
SK17 9DN

Tel: 01298 23628

Proprietors: Mr & Mrs V W Hesp

The Griff is a friendly, family run guest house. It is situated near the town centre but is in a quiet location away from heavy traffic.

Within 5-10 minutes walk you can be at the shops, in the town centre, at Poole's Cavern, outside the Opera House or in the beautiful Pavilion Gardens. We have 6 rooms, all are en-suite. Single, double, twin and family rooms available.

We are easy to find and there is ample parking space both outside the house and off the road.

Tariff:	Bed & breakfast	£ 25
	3 course evening meal:	£ 10 per head
	Main course only	£ 5 per head

Advance booking: Deposit £ 10 per person.
(£5 for children aged 2-12)